The Actor's Startup Guide

Six Ways To Land Your First Acting Job

Chris Agos

Cover design by ebooklaunch.com

ISBN: 979-8-9881753-1-5

Contents

About Chris Agos

Chris Agos launched his acting and voice over career in 1995. He quickly developed a reputation for efficiency and professionalism on the job, resulting in a career spanning thousands of projects. He has been cast in TV shows across various networks and streaming services, appeared in hundreds of commercials, and has been the voice of dozens of brands.

In 2007, he began teaching actors how to develop sustainable careers. That pursuit resulted in several books, including *The Voice Over Startup Guide, Acting in Chicago, Acting in Chicago for Kids and Parents, and Commercial Voice Over Strategies.*

He continues to audition, work, and help others get what they want from the entertainment industry. A Chicago native, he lives in Los Angeles with his wife and their twin sons.

Follow:

On socials: @ChrisAgos

On YouTube: @ChrisAgosActor

Reels and VO demos: www.chrisagos.com

CHRIS AGOS

Downloads mentioned in this book: www.actingcareermentor.com

Learn Voice Over: www.complete-voiceover.com

Learn about acting in the Midwest: www.actinginchicago.com

Also By Chris Agos

- *The Voice Over Startup Guide: How to Land Your First VO Job*

- *Commercial Voice Over Strategies: Tell a Story, Land the Job*

- *Acting in Chicago, 4th edition*

- *Acting in Chicago for Kids and Parents: How to Launch and Grow a Young Performer's Career*

Author's Note

Well, the hardest part is over. You showed up, so yay for you! Now take a deep breath and prepare to engage sponge mode.

Learning about anything new can be a challenge, but acting is a little different. It grips us in ways that other things don't because it requires sharing ourselves with others, making it exciting, risky, and important on a lot of levels.

For some, the idea of acting for a living is a little forbidden, too impractical to do as a career yet impossible to abandon. For others, it's a job they've always wanted and for whatever reason, now's the time. There's also the urge to create, to tell stories that feel important. Some people are just curious about acting and want to see where it can take them. And others have an even simpler reason why they want to perform: when they're acting, they're having buckets of fun.

Whatever's behind it, becoming an actor is a very personal journey. Everyone's path is different. Common to each are potholes, hairpin turns, and unexpected roadblocks. Finding our path of least resistance empowers us to make the journey shorter, smoother, and easier to navigate. That's what we're going to work on in this book.

In our digital era, getting started with something new usually begins with hopping online. Blogs, videos, pods, and social media give us glimpses of what we're looking for, but the truth is, that's a tricky way to learn about starting an acting career. Cobbling together knowledge from dozens of sources (some of them more reliable than others) can lead to more questions than answers.

Maybe you've experienced this yourself. Have you scrolled through content put out by casting directors? Sent DMs to podcast guests, hoping they'll answer your questions? Watched videos on self-taped auditions? These can be great resources, but what you learn comes to you randomly. Learning this way is the slow track.

Think of this book as the fast track, a way of having a well-organized, transformative process for launching your professional acting career. There's a lot to know, but my goal is to make it manageable. The industry is like a machine, of which actors are just one part. I'll share stories, provide some context, and drop a whole lot of pro tips that will make the machine work more smoothly for you.

The old barriers to joining the acting profession have been crumbling recently. You no longer have to live in any particular city or run with any particular crowd. You don't need to be in a specific age range or have a theater degree. You don't need to be willowy like a supermodel, be hilariously funny, or possess the ability to cry on cue. You can just be you.

So what, then, does an emerging actor need at the beginning of their journey? When I was new, I just wanted someone to tell me how to do this. I've been at it now for over twenty-five years, but I stumbled around for the first four or five of them. Mistakes were made. My first was thinking that if I was a good actor, I would work, end of story. That turned out to be an oversimplification.

It's one thing to know how to build a character in a story, but it's another thing to know how to build a career that lasts. Being a good actor is important, obviously. But unfair as it is, brilliance does not automatically equal staying power. There are just too many moving parts.

I'd like to help you stick around a while. In our time together, you'll learn about corners of the business, tiers of the business, and tools of the business. I'll explain basics, introduce advanced topics, and we'll have an honest talk about money. You'll learn how to manage expectations, apply an organized approach to your pursuit, and begin to find your path of least resistance. Whether you see acting as your calling or simply a creative side hustle, what you'll learn will allow you to spend less time figuring out the details and more time pursuing what you love.

Those twenty-five years taught me a lot. I am certainly not famous, but I have a work history some would envy. I launched my career in Chicago, where I made a full-time living for over two decades. I eventually moved to Los Angeles, where I've been fortunate enough to expand my career. This allowed me to work on a little of everything, from projects with the lowest of budgets and visibility to the highest. I've guest-starred on TV shows, made hundreds of commercials, spent more time than I ever thought I might as the face and voice of a major brand, and gotten to work with people I never thought I'd meet. Along the way I've helped thousands of emerging actors through my classes and the books I've written (*The Voice Over*

Startup Guide, Commercial Voice Over Strategies, Acting in Chicago, 4th edition). Through it all I lived a very normal life, financed by doing something I love.

I wish I could say all of it was easy and fast, but that's just not true. Despite what you may hear, there's no such thing as an overnight success in this industry. Actors have to work hard for their opportunities. This business weeds out people who are allergic to things like grit and persistence. It rewards those who thrive on the need to constantly improve, and to finish a job that was started. If that describes you, we've got a lot of work ahead of us.

Here's how we'll do it: this book is divided into four parts: The Work, The Tools, The Relationships, and The Money. Each subject could easily fill a whole volume, but I tried to keep them manageable. Read them in order because the later ones rely on previous information.

At the end of each section is a list of things you can do right now, wherever you are. It doesn't matter if you're completely untrained or returning to the business after a hiatus. It doesn't matter if you live in a world-class city or at the end of the dustiest rural road. There are things you can do *right now* that can help you move forward.

Remember, every actor's path is different. I don't expect you to do what I did or even follow the breadcrumbs I'll lay out. I do expect that you'll make some discoveries and find some inspiration here, and apply it on your own timeframe. That's how actors learn. We keep the ideas that resonate with us and leave the rest.

Our focus will be on establishing a career in recorded media. Performers wanting stage careers will still find value in these pages, but I'm sure there are other resources to explore.

This book is written from my perspective, and the best way to read it is with an open mind. If something strikes you as contrary to what you've heard or been told, it doesn't mean either view is wrong. It just means the two don't align. I don't have all the answers, but I really enjoy sharing what I've learned thus far.

I also like efficiency, so we'll move pretty quickly. If you find yourself wanting more, there are additional resources at actingcareermentor.com. The site is new and feels like it'll never be complete, so maybe check in once in a while for new information.

One more thing: learning how to get started in the acting profession is separate from collecting the skills needed to actually do the job. Although this book contains helpful guidance on training centers, it leaves the actual instruction up to the talented teachers running them.

We can only make good decisions if we have a complete picture of the world into which we're walking, so do me a favor and finish the book. It's easy to get sidetracked, but I firmly believe that more knowledge makes actors more confident. Lack of confidence is a killer, so we want to arm ourselves with enough of it to feel good about what we're doing.

Ready? Let's go.

Part 1

The Work

Chapter One

Looking For More

It's 6:00 a.m. and I've been awake for a couple of hours. The calendar says it's spring, but winter in Chicago never seems to loosen its grip on the city's mornings until well into June. I've got a hot cup of coffee in my hand and a full-length, fleece-lined warming coat draped over my wardrobe for the day, a new suit and stellar purple tie. The costume department always takes good care of me.

I walk up to a windowless trailer. It's about the size and shape of an eighteen-wheel big rig except no one would ever mistake it for one. With its bump-outs and retractable stairs, it looks more like an oversized motor home wrapped in glossy white cladding. The thing is easily bigger than my first house. I step onto the stairs and grab the door handle. It looks and feels like a big seatbelt buckle, the kind you'd click into place on an airplane, and it's frosty. My fingers slip right off. The spring-loaded flap slaps back with a loud *Thwack!*

It's production day number one of a new episode of a procedural drama that's a winner with TV audiences. For me and the character I play, it's our sixteenth episode, but it could also be our last. I'm not a regular on the show, meaning I'm onscreen only here and there, never really knowing when my character will be included in an episode or written out of the show entirely. Because of this, I make it my mission to enjoy every minute they let me spend on set.

I try the handle again and it rejects me a second time, sounding like a loud, steely exclamation point. But before I have a chance to give it another go, the door opens. A smiling makeup artist says, "We've been having trouble with this thing all morning. Come on in!"

Inside the makeup trailer it's bright and warm, and there's music playing. Three stylists are prepping and primping actors seated in their swiveling makeup chairs. There's an extremely fine mist of something, maybe steam or hairspray, wafting through the air. The makeup mirrors are framed with snapshots of the stylists' families and pets, along with the occasional closeup of a bloody wound. The show is a crime drama and people get shot, stabbed, burned, and otherwise maimed every week. It's up to the makeup crew to make it all look real, and this group is good.

High up near the ceiling is a row of faces, some smiling, others serious. It's the show's cast. All the actors in the episode are there, from the names you know to the ones you've never heard of. The regular players stay up on the wall the whole season, but the other photos rotate as guest cast members come and go.

One catches my eye because it's not a normal actor headshot, but a picture of a celebrity at a red carpet event. He's a special guest star in this episode, and I've seen him on movie screens since I was a kid. Today, I'll get to work with him.

A chair opens up and I take a seat, slipping my dress shoes onto the footrest. I bounce my knee up and down in an attempt to warm up faster, but it doesn't work. During the few minutes it takes the stylist to do my face, we chat about our weekend. I tell her about my kids, and she complains about her kitchen remodel, which is taking forever. I ask, "When it's finished, are you ever going to be home to enjoy it?" She smiles wanly and replies, "I know, right?" Production crews work notoriously long hours.

My next stop is one of the hair chairs, where a different stylist grabs a pair of clippers and goes to town on the nape of my neck. One of the best things about working in TV is the free haircuts. Sometimes a few months pass between my episodes and I come in looking shaggy, so they touch me up.

Switching to scissors, she swings around to snip above my forehead. I close my eyes to prevent having to pick the tiny trimmings out of them. Not only is that uncomfortable but it would disturb the makeup, forcing the previous stylist to fix it. That would make her mad. Pro tip: Never upset the person in charge of making you look good.

I hear the door handle's *Thwack!* Someone goes to the door with a sarcastic snort, clearly fed up with the broken thing. They pop it open and the trailer bounces gently as the newcomer climbs the stairs. He's greeted with a chorus of "Heyyyyy!" from the stylists.

I can't see what's going on, but it's obvious whoever arrives is well-liked. A deep male voice says, "Nice to see everybody again, nice to be here," as he makes his way down the narrow aisle.

I hear him settle into the chair next to me, so I crack one eye open. Past the little bits of hair dropping through my vision is the man from the red carpet photo, the one I grew up watching. He's sitting there, looking at me.

"Hi, I'm (insert celebrity name here)," he says. "You're Chris."

Comfort and makeup be damned, I open both eyes. I am all about acting like you've been there before, especially when it comes to luminaries. When I encounter them, I treat them like people. They put their pants on one leg at a time just like me and you, so I don't usually get weird around them. But in this case, all I could squeak out was, "Yeah." My admiration for the guy has caught up with me, but I am also thrown by the fact that he knows who I am. Then he really pulls the needle across the record and says, "Tell me about the chicken business."

One of the things you do when you're an actor is think about your online presence. That's where a lot of industry people first encounter you, so it's good to have a strategy for how you'll present yourself. There are all the usual social platforms to think about, but one of the resources most used by the industry is the Internet Movie Database, or IMDb.com. Actors have profiles there, though they're not nearly as customizable as those on other platforms. One thing we can do is write our own bios.

When you're a big shot, someone does that for you. I'm not even a medium shot, so I had to write my own. I hate boring bios. Don't you find it more interesting when you learn unexpected, offbeat things about people?

Readers of my profile will learn that when I was growing up, ours was the house that chicken built. My parents owned and operated a fried chicken restaurant. Yet as I was sitting in the hair chair, stumped,

IMDb was the furthest thing from my mind. I didn't understand why he mentioned chicken. The stylist gave me a little nudge. "What's he talking about?"

I shrugged and he continued. "I looked you up and want to know if the chicken business is good. There's a restaurant I'm thinking about buying because they always have lines out the door. They've got great food, but I don't know anything about that business. I figured you'd know."

At this point my confusion gave way to amazement. This person was a household name and Hollywood legend. He had spent more time in front of a camera than I'd been alive. He had absolutely earned the right to walk into work without doing anything more than reading the script, but he did his homework and researched the actors he would be working with.

So there we are, a couple of guys shrouded in makeup capes, chatting about chicken. I explain that my family no longer owned the restaurant but that it was very good to us when I was young. He shares that he likes to do his research before investing in something new to him. It's turning out to be a fantastic icebreaker since we're going to spend the rest of the day working together.

But as I walk back to my trailer, I think, "Why would a hugely successful actor want to do anything except act?" A lot of us spend no small amount of time and effort trying to convince the industry to let us work. When you finally have your pick of projects, what's interesting about a chicken place?

Chapter Two

Six Ways To Land Your First Job

A ctors have been branching out for decades. First there was the "triple threat," a term used to describe talent who are exceptional actors, singers, and dancers. If you could do all three well, you could stay employed forever. These artists have kept Broadway audiences dazzled for generations, and will continue to do so long into the future.

Then Paul Newman got into salad dressing, launching a nonprofit and turning his name into a staple supermarket brand. Eventually the idea of the entrepreneurial actor was taken much further. There are actors who invest in tech startups, lifestyle companies, soccer teams, and tequila brands. Many, many performers parlay their success into outside businesses.

Why, at the height of a career, switch focus? Why put time, talent, and money behind something wholly unrelated to acting? I'm sure there's more than one answer, but sitting in my trailer that cold spring morning, a single word popped into my head: diversification.

In finance, diversification is used to manage risk. In a volatile environment, it's a bridge to relative safety. When you have some money burning a hole in your pocket and you want it to grow, the list of places where you can invest it is endless. Choices range from blue chip stocks to the sketchy crypto/NFT/vaporware of the moment. If you put it all into one investment vehicle, your fortune rises and falls with that one thing. If the stock goes up, your money grows with it. If the crypto thingamajig goes to zero, your funds vanish. There's inherent risk in any investment, but having it all in one place is considered especially risky.

If instead you spread that money between a few stocks, a bond mutual fund, and maybe put a little in that crypto pipe dream, your whole nest egg would be much less impacted by a steep drop in one of them. Your other investments would cushion the fall. That's diversification in action.

If there is a holy grail to building a sustainable acting career, it's diversification. When you think of your career as your total investment, and your talent and skills as the actual dollars, you can see my point. Spreading those skills around multiple areas of opportunity makes you much less likely to be impacted by a downturn in any one of them. You're much more likely to have a stable income across your career and stay afloat in tough times. You want to diversify, especially early on.

Not all of us can start a makeup brand or open a restaurant, but any actor can build a career around the idea of diversification. The first step is to be open to the idea. Many performers come into the business with a predefined notion of what they want their career to look like. They have dreams, turn them into goals, and focus tirelessly on them. There is nothing wrong with that approach.

But consider that the world of acting offers more than just the thing you've dreamed of since you were a kid. I'm not saying you shouldn't aim high; I'm saying you should remain open to any and all opportunities as you're doing so.

The second step is to educate yourself about the ways actors are paid to use their skills. There's a whole world of work available to actors. Just as there is no single way to interpret and perform a scene, there is no single way of building an acting career. In the same vein, there's no single path all actors can rely upon to lead them where they want to go. Everyone's path is different. When it forks, you might go in one direction, and I might go in another.

You can only make an educated decision on which way to go if you know what your options are. The third step to career diversification is to explore all the ends of the business you uncover, pick one that speaks to you, and go for it. When you reach a point where you feel established in that area, try another one. Rinse and repeat.

Diversification doesn't mean letting go of your dreams, or taking your eye off the ball when it comes to what you really want to do. If your goal is to star in the next big superhero movie or award-winning TV series, do not let go of that. Diversification is not a compromise. Instead, it buys us time. A diversified career helps keep us in the game while we're working on our long-term goals.

Let's get into the six ways you can begin working as a professional actor. People are creative. They find their way into this business a million different ways. These six are not the only areas in which actors work, but I believe they are the most reliable and repeatable for the largest number of us. They have the added benefit of being doable everywhere, meaning we can participate no matter where we live. You know what some of them are, but others might be new to you.

TV/Film

I'm sure most readers have been inspired to become actors by watching their favorite TV shows and movies. The (good) actors in these projects make it seem so easy, don't they?

When we think of TV and film production, Los Angeles and New York probably come to mind. In the US, these cities are the two central hubs of the entertainment industry, but smaller cities and rural areas get in on the action, too.

In the past, casting had lofty expectations for actors who wanted even small roles. Actors with training from big-name schools were moved to the front of the line. Now, realism is prioritized over pedigree, making TV and film wide open to actors of all experience levels. If an actor looks and sounds like the character, they have a fighting chance at landing the role even without a fancy university on their resume. One casting director I spoke with said, "I don't need them to have gone to Juilliard if I'm casting Cheerleader #2."

Of course, the more visible a character is, the higher the expectations for what the actor can bring to it. Actors cannot stink up the joint and expect to be hired. We still have to deliver an impactful performance that's appropriate for what we read on the page, but it's good that the business has become more open to actors without a traditional education.

One of the challenges of working in TV and film is that each role has specific age and type requirements. To get an audition, an actor has to not only match up with them but also be known to the casting folks. If casting doesn't know you, you'll need someone they do know to pitch you for the role. More on this later.

Commercials

You know them. You might not love watching them. But when you appear in one, you will love the paycheck. Commercials (also called "spots") are a good source of employment for actors. I've done hundreds, and I hope to do hundreds more.

I think it's important to understand where an actor fits into the process of making a spot, so let's look at a simplified example from start to finish. A commercial starts with a product or service that needs some publicity. Maybe it's a new car. The car is made by a company, which hires an advertising agency to market the car. The ad agency assembles something called a "creative team," and they talk with the car company about what kind of image the car should have, who the target buyer might be, and ultimately decide how the car will be marketed.

Then the team conceives a few ideas for the campaign, and presents them to the car company. During this process, multiple concepts for commercials are discussed. When one is agreed upon, a script is written and submitted for approval by the car company.

Let's say it gets the green light for production. The ad agency then hires a production company, which is a firm that specializes in the production of commercials and other content, hence the name. They work with the ad agency to make sure the spot comes out exactly as it was pitched to, and approved by, the car company. They hire the crew (a director, set designers, a props department, etc.) and they also need a cast of actors.

The production company holds an audition, usually run by a casting director. The casting director is hired by the production company, and their job is to sort through all the talent (meaning actors) that might be right for the spot, have them audition, and present the results to the production company and the ad agency, who will decide (sometimes with the input of the client) which actors to use. Once the actors are cast, the spot gets made, aired, and then retired when it's no longer needed.

We'll talk more about casting directors and auditions later, but producing a spot is a complex job and involves a lot of money spent before actors ever get involved. Commercials are open to all ages and types of actors: young, old, beefy, skinny, quirky, studly, intellectual, goofy, and everything in between. After working in this business for a while, actors realize they fit into a "type" like "college kid," or "young mom." Your type will depend a lot on your age and how you present yourself, but there's work for every type out there, from creepy to wholesome.

Commercials are made all across the country and at all budget levels. There are spots with $1,000 budgets and accounts with millions of dollars at their disposal. These projects can be especially lucrative for actors who are members of a performance union, which we'll learn about later.

Industrials

Industrials are video productions produced by companies for certain purposes. Sometimes they pitch products, but they're often used to inform instead of promote. They are longer than spots and are often not intended to be seen by the general public.

Let's say an insurance company needs to teach new agents how to sell their policies. There are lots of ways to learn how to sell insurance, and one of those ways is to watch it being done. A training video might be made with scenes between an insurance agent and a customer. A script is carefully written to make sure the agent in the video is following all the company's rules and procedures, and the customer is responding realistically. Then, actors are hired to play out the scenes, which are shot, edited, and made available to the company's new hires.

You might wonder why the company doesn't use their own sales-people in these videos. Sometimes they do, but these folks are not actors. They can seem uncomfortable delivering a script in front of a camera. We've trained for that, they haven't, so companies hire professional actors to get professional results.

Just as in film and TV, actors who match the age and vibe of the role are usually cast. How the company projects itself to clients and customers also matters. Actors who have a more buttoned-up look and feel will work for companies that project that image (like banks). Conversely, a motorcycle maker is more likely to hire actors who look more at home working with tools. This goes back to actors having a "type."

Industrials, also referred to as corporate work, are produced everywhere for every kind of industry. I've shot for banks, tech firms, law firms, media companies, healthcare organizations, engine manufacturers, investment firms, consumer product makers, airlines, fast food places, car repair shops, retail stores, and on and on. These projects can be low-hanging fruit for actors because fewer of us are asked to audition for them than for a TV show or a commercial. Also, in contrast to other types of media, the message is the most important thing about an industrial, not the actor delivering it. This means that actors who are good at delivering these types of scripts will always be in demand, even if they're not exactly right for the job.

Voice Over

When you watch a project and a voice is heard but not seen, you're listening to a voice over (VO). People who do this type of work are called either "voice overs," "voice actors," or "voice talent." Any way you say it, you could be rolling in dough if you decide to stay off camera.

Voice over is used in all kinds of media: TV, radio, film, commercials, industrials, web, video games, toys, and audiobooks. I was even the voice of a treadmill. A fitness company made a machine that offered a virtual personal trainer to help motivate you through your workouts. Users could pick between a male or female trainer, and I was the voice of the guy.

Whenever I teach VO, there's always someone in class who says, "I've been told I have a good voice and that I should do this." And my reply is always, "That's great, but what you sound like doesn't matter nearly as much as what you can do with a script." It used to be that voice talent were required to have a "radio voice," one that was male, deep, and resonant. Now the gender gap has closed and there's room for all voice types.

If you've never had a VO lesson before, here's your first one. If I say the word "announcer," what kind of image comes to mind? Most people picture an older gentleman talking into a microphone holding one hand up to his ear, using a booming voice that virtually commands us to pay attention. But those days and those announcers are long gone. Today's announcers, men and women representing all ethnicities, have everyday-sounding voices. And advertisers have ditched the false authority in favor of a more conversational style. So never, ever approach a voice over job from the standpoint of a "traditional" announcer, unless of course you're asked to do just that. There is a lot more to VO, and if you're interested in getting a more complete introduction to it, check out my book *The Voice Over Startup Guide: How to Land Your First VO Job.*

VO has been essential to my ability to make a living, but there are some barriers to getting started. While actors make great voice talent, it's a completely different skill set than others we might have, so training is a must. Also, a home studio is required for all of today's voice talent because it's essentially a home-based business. All our auditions are done from home, as is the majority of our paying jobs. Setting up a studio can be daunting, so in addition to writing

The Voice Over Startup Guide, I've put together a free VO resource guide to make the process simpler. It's available to download at ActingCareerMentor.com.

A word of caution: there are some folks whose chances for VO work will be extremely limited. If you speak English with an accent either because it's your second language or because you have a strong regionality, you'll only be eligible for work that requires the accent. Talent with speech impediments should work with a therapist to mask as much of it as possible before pursuing VO.

The bottom line is VO can be a lucrative addition to your actor toolbox, but it takes specific training to be able to do it well. The good news is that there's a lot of money to be made in this work category. We'll get very specific about what voice talent can earn in a later chapter.

Commercial Print

The term "print" covers any job where an actor's photograph is taken with a still camera. The term "commercial" means that the image is used to promote a product or service. It might be used in online ads, product packaging, mailers, point-of-purchase displays, billboards, or anything else that can display a picture.

You might think that models, not actors, are used for this kind of stuff. Sometimes they are, but ad agencies also like to use "real people," the term they use to describe folks who look like the guy who delivers your packages or the girl who rings up your groceries.

For obvious reasons, this work is all about how you look. The acting thing is secondary, though it still counts because all print jobs are going after some kind of "feel" the model must emote. You might need to be really excited, confident, or confused, and you've got to be able to connect with that state of mind and actually look like you're excited, confident, or confused.

A number of years ago, a friend of mine got a print job that took place on location in a bowling alley. These days, actors have test shots posted in online galleries for potential clients to view. But back then, we went to auditions where they snapped Polaroids of us and delivered them to the client in a box. When my friend showed up at the job, she happened to walk by the table the client was using to organize the paperwork for the job, and she spotted her Polaroid. On it, written in small handwriting, was "Looks like a bowler." That's why she got the job. She didn't know what that meant, the fact that someone thought she looked like a bowler, but she was happy to have the cash.

Print jobs occasionally come as a bonus with on-camera work. I once did a series of TV spots for a medical association, and they also wanted to use my image in a print campaign. My agent negotiated a separate fee for the print component because the TV shoot only entitled them to use my likeness for that purpose. This means I was paid twice, once for each use.

Print jobs are great because they're usually quick and pay fairly well. The downside is that it takes longer to get paid for print work for a variety of reasons, one of which is that it's not covered by a union. More on that subject later.

Trade Shows/Live Events

Trade shows are conventions where companies from a specific industry, like construction equipment makers or medical device manufacturers, gather to show their new products. Companies rent booth space on the floor of convention centers and spend huge amounts of money styling them to best reflect their agenda at the show. The pandemic slowed this industry to a crawl, but business has bounced back.

A trade show offers several different opportunities for working actors. Companies hire hosts, crowd gatherers, product specialists, and presenters. A host's job often involves handing out promotional items or checking show attendees into the booth if they have appointments. Being a crowd gatherer requires chatting with people and encouraging them to visit the booth. Product specialists are trained by the client to speak about their product or service one-on-one with show attendees. Presenters speak in front of large groups, delivering the company's main message for the show.

Hosts, crowd gatherers, and product specialists come from all walks of life. Clients like to hire whoever can easily strike up a conversation with a stranger. All trade show employees are expected to interact with the public, so people skills are a must.

If you are, or look and behave like you're at least twenty-five years old and are good with public speaking, then you could be a candidate to be a presenter. Just like with industrials, companies like to hire actors that fit the company's image.

Presenters are often required to use a handy tool called an ear prompter. It's like a teleprompter for your ear. Instead of reading and reciting a scrolling script, we hear the script in an earpiece that is invisible to the audience. As the audio rolls, we recite the words we hear. It's a specific skill that requires some practice and is also sometimes used on camera, mostly in industrial work.

Trade shows have pluses and minuses for actors. On the one hand, they tend to require more working days than commercials or industrials. Where one of those jobs could be done in as little as a few hours, a trade show could run four or five days, making them pretty lucrative. What's more, sometimes a company will hire you to do multiple shows, meaning you can count on having consistent work throughout the year. The downside is that you may not be included on any auditions back home when you're gone. You might get a self-tape (more on this later), but you could also miss something really great. At least you'd be working, though, which is the whole goal.

Chapter Three

Diversification Details

S ome of these acting disciplines might sound fantastic, others not so much. Why would an actor consider working in any of these areas besides TV and film? Most people don't grow up dreaming of being in a corporate video or pizza commercial.

A career can be impacted by events large and small, so it's important to do what we can to smooth out any bumps. I'm sure it won't be a surprise to hear that many actors struggled during the pandemic. Literally overnight, their way of making a living vanished. For people whose careers revolve around drama, this was the kind no one wanted.

Except there was a group who not only survived, but actually thrived during this time. They saw their incomes stay the same or even grow because they worked in an area of the business that didn't shut down: voice over.

VO is a huge industry on its own, one that embraced working from home over a decade ago. Pre-pandemic, about 90 percent of VO auditions and half of all jobs were already being done in home studios. The pandemic pushed both numbers to near 100 percent. So except for a brief hiccup in March 2020 when it seemed like the entire world shut down, voice talent kept on working as if nothing had happened.

Voice actors also thrived during the summer of 2023 when Hollywood's unions were striking against movie and TV studios. The labor stoppage brought live action TV and film work to a screeching halt, but voice talent continued working in animation, commercials, gaming, audio book narration and other areas of VO because none of that work was included in the strike.

Actors should take every opportunity to insulate themselves from unpredictable events. The best way to do that is to be prepared to adjust when things change. In this business, people come and go, trends shift, and tastes evolve quickly. Diversification makes it far easier to roll with all of it, and keep going.

Look at different areas of the business as tools that can help you achieve your long-term goals. You don't have to love them or be creatively fulfilled by them, but you will appreciate them when they help keep your bank account full enough, your confidence high enough, and your stamina healthy enough to stay in this business over the long term.

Each acting discipline represents a market of its own. They are their own little worlds, having specialized purposes and unique audiences, with separate protocols and talent buyers. A producer of a TV show doesn't care how many commercials you've done, and a VO casting director won't want to know how many trade shows you've worked. Our goal is to easily cross from one discipline to another so when an unexpected macro event comes along, like a pandemic or the hot labor summer of 2023, our income can remain relatively stable.

The Rules

There are a couple of rules to this diversification thing. They're simple, but important.

The first is about intent. We have to make the decision to approach our career in this way. Without that decision, we're likely to get distracted. There are plenty of other ways to develop an acting career. Consciously deciding to choose this path can allow us to develop and execute a plan instead of bouncing from one approach to another.

The second rule is that it only works if an actor commits to it. It's just like building a character. One critical part of our scene work is to make choices about the character we're playing. Then, we stick to them. We don't play them in one part of a scene and ignore them in another unless the script calls for that. We see those choices through the entire scene, or play, or television season. If you don't commit to your choices, the character doesn't ring true for the audience. Same thing with diversification. If you're going to expand your horizons, do so. Know that it will take time, and that it may be uncomfortable. But it may also lead to important discoveries, so the benefits outweigh the risks.

The third rule is that actors are not required to do it all, but they should be willing to *try* it all. If you're feeling overwhelmed, you'll be relieved to know that most of us don't do it all. We gravitate toward a handful of things that make sense for us, but we can't find them without a willingness to try as many as possible.

Take each area of the business one at a time. Start with the one that seems most interesting. Go slow. There's no need to become an expert in every area right away. Trying to learn it all simultaneously can be expensive and lead to burnout. It's also not a good idea to be the actor who's familiar with everything, but not really good at anything. So get to know a skill, master it, then explore the next.

There are multiple benefits to this strategy. Working in these six corners of the industry will allow us to find our strengths and weaknesses. We'll discover things that come easily to us, and ones that are really challenging. Trying everything makes us ready for anything.

The Path of Least Resistance

There's more than stability involved in varying our skill sets. Diversification allows us to start finding our path of least resistance through the larger industry. You're smart, so you know there are no guarantees in this business. Friction exists in many forms. One way to ease it is to uncover what we bring to the party, and lean into it.

In fact, I think the most exciting thing about exploring all your options as an actor is this: you might be really good at something you would never have considered if you weren't looking for new tools to add to your tool box.

I'll give you an example. I did a lot of corporate narration. I appeared on camera as a spokesperson for hundreds of companies, talking about everything from home repair to printing presses. A narrator's job is not to understand what we're saying, but to appear as though we do. When we narrate, the audience sees us as experts talking about something with which we're very familiar. If we can't live up to that expectation, we don't get much narration work.

I accidentally discovered that I had a natural gift for looking and sounding like I knew what I was talking about when I in fact had *no idea* what I was talking about. I wasn't trying to get into narration, but when I kept booking the work, I didn't turn it down. In fact, once I discovered that it paid well and didn't take up a lot of time, I did the opposite and made it my survival job. If you're curious about the numbers, we'll get very specific about how much you'll earn for each type of work in a later chapter.

There's a risk/reward calculation involved in starting an acting career. What we're risking is the time, money, and effort we'll put into it. The reward we're looking for is a successful career that lasts. That becomes more attainable when we find ways to work that line up with what we naturally offer just by being who we are.

Once you've acknowledged the desire to diversify your career and made the decision to get started, you'll need to do some learning. Let's talk about that next.

Chapter Four

Training

A ctors who make the job look easy have trained hard. Everyone has a certain amount of natural talent, but it takes instruction to put it to use. Besides that, actors need to know the language used by the industry, and we learn a lot of it in our training.

What classes you take and where you take them will depend on several factors: whether you come from an acting background, what kind of work you want to explore, and what skills you'll need to develop to work in those areas. If you're new to acting, you'll need an intro-level class. This will hopefully give you a good foundation on which to build.

If you're not exactly new but you've never worked at a profession-al level, there are classes aimed at students who have done some performing and have a general grasp of the fundamentals. Typically these classes revolve around scene study, where you and a partner analyze and perform a scene from a play, TV series, or film. For the actor whose experience has been limited to only high school or college stages, these classes can be a real eye-opener, giving them a chance to work with partners of all ages.

Actors with a good amount of training will enter ongoing classes, which are often offered by schools as a way to practice and keep sharp. They can vary wildly depending on the policies of the schools and their style of teaching. Some require auditions for admittance, and others are closed to anyone other than students who have studied in the school's lower-level classes.

Choosing a Training Center

The task of training actors mostly falls to two groups of institutions: colleges and universities, and independent acting schools. Plenty of actors come from the former, and an equal amount (or maybe even more) lean on the latter to teach them the skills they'll need to become professionals. There are some things to keep in mind when considering either.

Actors who want an undergraduate degree in theater arts or an MFA (master of fine arts) attend a college or university. These are four-year programs (typically two years for an MFA), require attendance full time, and are quite expensive. Given their immersive nature, they're not practical for most working adults. It's pretty rare for someone to drop everything and interrupt their family life to get a theater degree.

There are some things you should expect if you're considering going this route. Students are generally immersed in theater, and study everything from theater history to production. Instructional materials run the gamut from classical pieces to modern masters. Colleges are often where new scripts are workshopped, meaning students get to originate characters and help playwrights refine their ideas.

Different acting techniques are offered up, giving students several options for expression. This can be a kind of buffet-style approach, where actors get a sample of everything. Not every technique will resonate with every actor, so it's a good way to find what works. Some programs will also blend in musical theater, and still others are completely focused on it.

Many collegiate programs don't incorporate much film or television into their curriculum, though that's starting to change. Also, stage time can be limited for newer students, as those who are further along in the program get most of the performance opportunities. Schools usually don't allow enrolled actors to work during their studies. You might also expect to take some general courses unrelated to theater to complete your degree unless you attend a conservatory where that's not a requirement.

If we're past our college years or want another option, the more practical solution for learning about the business lies with independent acting studios. These schools are much more affordable than colleges, and students can come and go as their time and budgets allow. Usually owned and run by performers (or former performers), you won't get a degree, but that doesn't mean you can't get a great education in these places.

It's very common for an acting studio to teach the tools and techniques embraced by their founders. When a studio owner has a strong belief in a certain method, they tend to pass it on to their students. In places like this, you're unlikely to get exposure to other ways of doing things unless you try multiple schools. That's neither good nor bad, but it's good to be aware of. Usually, schools tell prospective students if they follow a certain acting technique, so check their websites to be sure.

Other studios don't rely on an established training method and instead teach their own way of doing things. These methods may come from observations, experiments, experience, and conversations with other industry professionals.

Schools may have a figurehead whose name is on the front door. As a student there, you're putting your trust in that person's interpretation of the profession. Again, this is neither good nor bad. Sometimes an actor will get more from a blend of techniques instead of just relying on one.

Many schools offer a little bit of everything. You'll find foundational classes, advanced classes, courses and camps for kids, ones on movement and voice, and on and on. On the other end of the spectrum, you'll also find schools with very narrow class offerings. There are also places that describe themselves as schools of the performing arts, meaning they cover everything from musical instruments, to dance and other performance disciplines along with acting. If this is what's available near you, a school like this may be a fine place in which to get started. Ideally, though, you'll be able to find a place focused mostly on acting.

The pandemic ushered in the era of online acting classes. No matter where you live, you can now study with studios in New York, LA, Chicago, or anywhere else in the world. This is an amazing opportunity, but be aware that distance learning is not ideal. Online meetings lack the ability to connect with acting partners, and internet issues can ruin the experience pretty quickly. Many actors who have taken online instruction tell me they prefer to meet with their class in person, but it's a solid choice if there's no other option.

Online classes are offered in a couple of formats. The first is a pre-recorded version, where students watch instructors on video at their own pace. Basically, it's like learning how to do anything else online. You watch, then implement the techniques on your own. Missing from this equation is feedback from an instructor and working with a partner, which are critical elements of learning how to act.

Most actors, if they're going to take online classes, will opt for the other way to take them, where the class meets as a group over Zoom or some other videoconference app. This doesn't replace being in the room, but it closes the distance between people and is certainly better than nothing.

Things to Consider

When you're interested in a studio, it's good to find out if they teach a particular method. See if you can find a clear definition of its central aspects. There can be a lot of flowery language written about acting techniques, and you'll find vociferous disciples for every one of them. Try to push past this and tease out what you'll actually do in class. If you'll be pushing some uncomfortable boundaries, that's something you want to know in advance. Remember that acting is just listening and responding honestly. It's no more complicated than that.

Cost is a consideration. Buying access to a prerecorded video course should cost less than one taught in real time. You're giving something up for the convenience of taking a class this way, so make sure you're spending less to do it.

Classes generally cost a few hundred dollars each. This will vary depending on geography, how many schools are in the local area, and who's doing the teaching. Some schools offer a subscription model, where they charge a flat monthly rate for classes. Before you register for anything, make sure you understand how much it'll cost, and when and how it will meet. And of course, if you plan to enroll somewhere with a person's name above the door, make sure to google them before you do.

If you're planning on attending class in person, which I think you should try to do early in your training, ideally the school should be reasonably close to home. When I was teaching in Chicago, some students would drive in from as far away as Michigan. I applauded their determination, but was also worried for them every time they drove home late at night. Some of my students didn't make it home until the wee hours of the morning, then went to work the next day. I'm honored they thought the trade-off was worth it, but I'd advise anyone to avoid that kind of scenario if they can.

Perhaps the most important thing to consider at any training center is the faculty. I highly recommend vetting whomever you're going to trust to teach you. I'm a big fan of learning from people who have done what I'd like to do. Find the names of teachers on the school's site, then see if they have personal websites and if they do, look through them. Follow their social profiles. Then plug their names into IMDb.com and iSpot.tv and see what comes up. All of this should give you some sense of their work history. If you come up blank, it's possible the instructors have had careers in the theater. That's fine, but harder to verify.

Many schools tout the success of their students. There's nothing wrong with this, but be aware that it's a marketing technique called "social proof," and it's designed to impress you. The implication is that if you attend that school, you'll get the same results. Know that career success comes from many factors, not just where you study acting.

Red Flags

Sketchy marketing is one red flag that would make me pass on a school. If I get the impression they're working a little too hard to convince me of how great they are, or if their boasts seem farfetched, I'm going to look elsewhere.

Very high cost for classes is another red flag. There's no need to spend more than a few hundred dollars on a class, though you should expect to pay more in major metropolitan areas than you will in smaller towns.

Keep in mind there's certainly no need to take more than one class at a time. Some places like to sell class packages, resulting in actors spending a lot of money in a short period of time. That doesn't mean you're going to get a better education, faster. Some packages include extras like headshots and demo reels. I can't speak for every school that offers these services, of course, but you can assume they are revenue drivers for the school, and you may or may not get the results you want from them. We'll talk more about these things in a later chapter.

Finally, tread lightly around live conventions. Some companies like to advertise heavily on social media, come into smaller towns, and try to pack hotel ballrooms with actors (and parents of young performers) hoping to start careers. There, they typically use pushy sales techniques to get people to buy experiences, classes, and other stuff. I'm not here to judge, I'm just saying that the professional world ignores these things, which means that you probably should, too.

Legitimate live gatherings of actors do exist. I've been involved with them in the past and will likely do so in the future. Just check them out thoroughly before attending.

Coaches

Classes are one way to go, but for actors who want more individual attention, working with a coach can be a solution. This one-on-one experience is most effective when the actor has a clear goal in mind, such as working on a specific audition, getting ready to submit to a particular talent agency, or trying to level up in certain types of work.

My opinion is that there's a coach out there for everyone. The hard part is finding that person. Personally, I want two things from a coach: an innovative way of helping me reach my goal, and someone with whom I personally click. I've had coaches I respected a great deal as actors, but didn't really get along with. I've also had coaches I enjoyed hanging out with, but who didn't add much to my acting. Neither is ideal.

Coaches usually work by the hour, and prices can be all over the map. I've paid anywhere from $75 to $500 per hour. Those pricey folks were interesting, to say the least. I did not go back to them, but I was also glad for the experience. I'm going to guess that it's an LA or NYC thing to charge that much.

I would vet a potential coach just like I would a class instructor. Credibility is everything. Referrals from other actors are possibly the best way to find coaches.

Experience

You can't get experience without working, and you can't work without experience. Everyone in the industry understands the emerging actor's conundrum. All the training in the world can go out the window when you're on your first job, standing in front of a camera, and there are fifteen lights spotted on you, twenty people standing around watching your every move, and five of them are telling you what to do. Plus, maybe there's a celebrity on set. What is it that Mike Tyson says? "Everyone has a plan until they get punched in the mouth."

So how do you build some confidence? Taking classes is a start. When I was a new actor, taking a class was really my only viable option. There were no camera phones, and I couldn't afford a camcorder. My only alternative was to practice for class by reading scripts in front of a mirror. That worked (sort of), but what I really wanted was a setup where I could tape myself, play it back, and experiment with changing things up in the privacy of my own home.

Which brings me to my point. Your phone has a camera, so use it. Besides paying for time in front of a camera by taking a class, this is the best way to get familiar with performing in front of a lens. I think this option is most effective when it's done in conjunction with a class. The down side to studying on your own at home is that you've got no one but yourself to critique your performance. At this point in your development, you probably don't have the knowledge to know what changes you might make. Or worse, you may think you know what to change. Supplement the self-teaching method by enrolling in a course taught by a professional.

You might say, "Well, I'll just learn on the job." Believe me, you'll learn plenty when you're working. In fact, I think work experience beats class experience by a long shot. Directors, other actors, and crew members can provide a wealth of information and helpful tips you can tuck away and use later, but you want to have at least a little working knowledge before you're cast in a paying job. The key word there is "paying."

By the time you're on set, months (sometimes longer) have gone into planning the job, and lots of money has been spent. Concepts were pitched, scripts were written, locations were scouted, insurance was purchased, lawyers were consulted, crew was hired, equipment was rented, costumes were bought, travel arrangements were booked, and schedules were set. Very often the budget is so tight that every-thing must go according to plan. An eight-hour day just can't stretch into ten, because there's no money left to pay for overtime.

As actors, it's our job to make sure we don't cause any delays. We're expected to show up on time, know our stuff, and do the job well. Understandably, no one wants to pay you to learn on their set; they expect you to know what you're doing before they hire you. In fact, you probably gave them that exact impression in your audition! If it's clear that you can't live up to that expectation, there's a problem, and you will feel terrible about it as it's happening. Solve it by getting comfortable in class and practicing at home to get sharp.

The great thing about taking classes is that you're not just going to learn about the subject being taught, you're also going to pick up bits and pieces about other aspects of the business, like auditions. Let's talk about those next.

Chapter Five

Auditions

No matter how successful you become, it's likely that you'll always have to audition for work. Actors might audition less as we tap into repeat business, but being handed a job is usually reserved for very few performers. For everyone else, we need to show the decision-makers we're right for the role.

Auditioning is a critical skill, one separate from performing. We must be able to deliver an audition that makes sense for what we read on the page while giving it our own unique spin, and do it by a deadline.

For the entire history of auditions, the only way to do them was live and in person. Both actor and decision-maker would occupy the same physical space, be it an audition room or a theater, to determine whether that actor was right for a specific role. The pandemic ushered in a new era, one where actors produce their audition at home more often than they do in front of other humans. This trend had been slowly developing, but wasn't widely adopted until it had to be.

At this point, the industry seems to be trying to figure out when to use in-person auditions over self-tapes, and vice versa. Casting directors in TV and film are fine with self-tapes, and they dragged commercial CDs to the party, too, yet plenty of commercial auditions are still held in casting offices. Actors auditioning for VO jobs have been doing them from home for years. A lot of print work has cut back on live look-sees and has gone virtual. Industrial and trade show auditions still commonly happen in person. We'll cover many types of auditions so you know what to expect from all of them.

Useful Terminology

There are a handful of terms used during auditions that might be confusing when you first encounter them.

The first is "the room." This is is the literal room in which your audition takes place. When you're auditioning in person, you'll arrive and be asked to wait in a different room until they're ready to see you, at which point you'll head into the room where the audition will happen. If you're auditioning at home, the room likely refers to the virtual space where you'll connect with the person watching your audition. More on virtual auditions in a bit.

The second term is "slate." It's a holdover from the days when individual takes of scenes were labeled on camera by raising a chalkboard into the frame. On it would be written scene numbers and other information identifying what was about to appear, and it helped the film's editor keep everything organized.

In the context of an audition, the term is used to describe an actor identifying themselves. An actor's slate is simply them saying, "Hi, I'm (your name here)." Sometimes we're asked for a little more information, like how tall we are or what city we live in, but if anyone ever says, "Go ahead and slate," they just need to record you identifying yourself.

Next up is an actor's "mark." A mark is a specific location where we're asked to stand. It is literally a mark on the floor, usually made from tape and in the shape of a T. You place your feet to either side of the vertical part of the T and your toes on the horizontal part. Being on your mark means you're properly lit and can be easily seen by the camera. When you're told to "hit your mark," whether in an audition or on an actual job, you're being asked to stand in that spot or land there if you're walking into the shot.

Finally, when there's more than one character in an audition scene, you'll need a "reader." Readers are responsible for delivering the lines of all the other roles in a scene, the ones for which you're not auditioning. If the scene is between a husband and wife, a reader will read one of them while the actor who is auditioning will perform the other. Readers stay off camera, and are typically not in performance mode. After all, it isn't their audition, it's yours.

Good readers provide line readings the auditioning actor can work with without pulling focus from them. Other actors make the best readers, but in a pinch anyone can do it. Friends, spouses, acting coaches, or anyone willing to help can jump in. In some auditions, casting directors or their assistants are the readers.

Self-Taped Auditions

There are two types of at-home, or self-taped, auditions. The first is when you tape your audition without using a videoconferencing app. It's just you at home with your self-tape setup a reader. I call this a "stand-alone audition." In this case you slate, shoot the scene(s), edit the footage, and send it off to whoever asked for the audition. They'll view it later. With this type of audition, you can have as many takes as you need to get your performance how you want it, though you do have to be mindful of deadlines. As long as the file is submitted on time, it will be viewed by the client.

It's also possible to have a stand-alone audition with a virtual reader. This happens when no one's available to be there in the room with you. In cases like these, we still need someone to help us with the lines of any other characters in the scene. FaceTime or Zoom will allow your reader to help you in real time from wherever they are in the world. More on this in a bit.

The second type of audition happens when you dial into an audition through an app like Zoom or EcoCast Live, and someone from casting acts as your reader. This virtual audition is similar to an in-person audition in that it's run by casting and is recorded on their end, but they are not physically in the room with you. You're home, and they're in their office. They act as your virtual reader. In this case, you don't have unlimited takes and you don't have to do anything with the file after the audition is finished because it's being recorded on their end. When you log off, your audition is complete.

In a later chapter, we'll learn about putting together and using a solid self-tape setup.

Auditioning In Person

If you're new to auditioning in a professional environment, let's start at the beginning. Your agent will email you the audition details. You'll be told what the project is, what role you're auditioning for, and when your appointment is scheduled. You might also be given callback and shoot dates, which you should check against your calendar to make sure you're available. If you have a conflict with the dates, tell your agent. They'll either advise you to skip it or do the audition anyway to see what happens.

If you're not available at your scheduled audition time, let your agent know. They may or may not be able to get you another audition time, but it never hurts to ask. Whatever time you're given, try to make it work since rescheduling could lead to losing the chance to audition.

Let's assume you're available. A script will likely be attached to the email from your agent. On rare occasions the scripts aren't ready until the day of the audition, so you'll get them when you show up. This usually only happens if your role has very few lines. Most agents and casting directors try hard to get actors their scripts with plenty of time to prepare.

When you're auditioning for a role that has no lines at all, these are called "MOS auditions." MOS is an acronym, meaning the letters are pronounced individually, like when you say, "USA." It stands for "Mitt Out Sound," and no, that's not a typo. There's a bit of legend surrounding this, which involves a German director from the 1930s who spoke English with a heavy accent. I have no idea if the story is true or not, so I'll spare you the details. Just know that when you have an MOS audition, your character does not speak.

Once you have the necessary information, you should spend some time with however many scripts you're sent. If it's a commercial audition, there could be multiples, and if you're reading for a TV show or film, you might have multiple scenes from the project. It's important to know the material well. Some people will say your auditions have to be memorized, but I don't share that view. An audition is not a test of your memorization skills, though I have to admit that it looks pretty good if you're off book. Sometimes there isn't enough time to memorize everything, so in those cases feel free to hold the script in your hand. Better that than to have the words escape you.

Wardrobe

Give some thought to what you'll wear during auditions. Sometimes you'll be told exactly what the client would like to see. Other times, it'll be up to you. If you're left to figure it out on your own, look to the script for clues. You want to wear things that suggest the character. If you're reading for the part of a doctor, you'll probably need a nice button-down shirt. I once auditioned for a bank commercial, yet the role I was up for was that of a jogger. I showed up wearing my running clothes (newer ones, not old sweaty ones).

If you're not specifically told what to wear, there are three styles (or looks) that are often used as a general guideline:

- Professional. This means suits and ties for men, and suits or jacket/skirt combos for women. Think two lawyers arguing in a courtroom.

- Business casual/nice casual. Pants and button-down shirts for men and khakis or more casual skirts and nice tops for women. Think a nice night out on the weekend. Sometimes you can get away with jeans, but only if they aren't distressed or ripped.

- Casual. Whatever you'd wear around the house. Jeans and T-shirts or polos for the guys (but nothing with a logo or graphic on it), jeans and casual tops for the women. Think running errands or watching the big game with friends. Don't go too sloppy here. Make sure you're not wearing your grubbiest shirt unless you're asked to do so.

Whatever you wear, you'll need to follow a few rules. First and foremost, make sure your clothing choice is appropriate for the role. Follow the directions and if you're not given any, read the script and give it your best guess. Look to TV shows or commercials that have the same kind of setup as the one you're auditioning for and use what the actors are wearing as a starting point. Unless you're told otherwise, your wardrobe choice should be three things: in step with current style, age appropriate, and modest.

Second, stay away from anything that could be seen as a full-on costume. No need to go out and buy a set of surgical scrubs or a chef's uniform. Simply wear something that suggests these things. Same goes for hairstyles, which should make sense with the rest of the look.

Also, avoid stripes and bold patterns because cameras don't like them. The reason is a bit technical, but it comes down to how a camera's sensors process information. Stripes can sometimes produce an effect called a "moiré pattern," which are ripples or waves moving on the screen over the striped piece of clothing. This is distracting and you want the decision-makers to watch you, not your striped tie.

Cameras tend to like earth tones, warm colors, and soft pastels. Grays and jewel tones are nice, too. Red sometimes makes some skin tones look funny, so most actors skip it and go for more subdued colors.

Last, make sure there are no logos visible. If they're very small and unobtrusive, that's fine. But you want to leave your Nike or Supreme stuff in the closet. Oh, and don't forget your feet. Wear shoes that fit with the rest of your look. After a while, all of this will become second nature.

This all goes for auditions which happen on camera. Wear anything you want to your VO auditions!

Pro Tips for Auditioning In Person

On the audition day, get there on time. Being late may cost you the chance to audition. In my world, being on time means arriving fifteen minutes early so I can find parking and read any additional information that might be posted before my actual time slot. If you're auditioning at a casting director's office, there's sometimes a short info sheet to fill out including your wardrobe sizes and scheduling commitments (like other bookings) that might conflict with the shoot dates. If there are storyboards or other character descriptions posted, have a look at these, since they can be helpful.

After you're signed in and have read what there is to read, have a seat. Go through a mental checklist of what you've prepared to do in the audition room. Run through it once or twice in your head, and try to relax. When it's your turn, your name will be called. Bring yourself and your stuff into the room and do your best.

Let's talk about what you can expect from auditions for each type of work.

Commercials

Most in-person commercial auditions take place at a casting director's office, but some will happen at your agent's office or at an ad agency. At a casting director's office, there will likely be at least two people in the room to watch: the casting director and someone running the equipment. There may also be someone in another location watching the audition via video conference. At your agent's office, it might just be you and your agent. At an ad agency, there could be a whole bunch of people watching. In any case, you might be given some last-minute instructions that may or may not be completely different from what you were told before. In this business, minds change quickly and if there wasn't time to update the actors, they just do it at the audition.

The audition room will be arranged with the camera at one end, pointed at an audition area at the other end. If the spot requires a set, a very simple one will be there for you. I use the term "set" incredibly loosely. If the scene takes place at a table, there will be one there with enough chairs around it to accommodate everyone in the scene. If you need specific props for the spot, like if you're supposed to use a laptop, the casting director will provide one for you. Never bring your own props.

All auditions pretty much run the same way. Before the audition begins, they'll likely get your slate. When you're ready, you'll do the first take. You'll be told to make some changes and incorporate them into your second take. Based on how that goes, you may be asked to try some other options. Two or three takes usually is the most you'll get, then you're free to go.

Every actor in nearly every audition is asked to do multiple takes. Don't take this personally. You can't possibly know exactly what they're looking for before you go in, so do your best on the first take and let them direct you for the rest. It's how they bring you closer to getting the job.

The one exception to the multiple-take audition model is a style of audition that's closer to an interview. This is common when you're reading for the role of a character who does some kind of simple, everyday task in the spot. Anyone can wipe down windows or sit on a couch and watch a movie, so it's easier for producers to cast these kinds of roles by seeing actors' personalities instead of their mastery of mundane skills.

Sometimes interview questions can be related to the spot, like "Tell me about your experience with power tools." Or they can be totally random, like "What would you do if you won the lottery tomorrow?" In any case, producers just want to get a sense of who you are.

In a self-taped commercial audition, this will all happen at home without the help of a casting director. Instead, instructions will be emailed with the audition notice. Follow them to the letter to make sure your audition is complete. You wouldn't want to be eliminated from contention because you missed a detail.

Industrials

Auditions for industrials can take place at various locations: a casting director's office, your agent's place, or at the client's facility. They are run in much the same way as commercial auditions. You'll slate, then go into the prepared piece. A couple of changes, a second take, and you're out of there.

By the way, you should always expect to do the script at least twice. You may have nailed it on the first try, but even if you did, there's always some variation that clients will want to see. Many of them don't know exactly what they want, and they ask actors to help them find out. Their questions usually start with "What if," and the answer comes out in the changes we make to our reads. For example, "What if the situation was a little more tense?" This kind of thing is all part of the process.

Voice Over

VO auditions used to take place at your agent's office, ad agencies, or at recording studios. That was back in the day when voice talent actually saw each other. Now, we never see anyone because with few exceptions, everyone auditions and works at home. I miss the old days!

A home recording setup can be as simple as an iPhone and a closet, or as elaborate as a professionally designed booth with all the fancy tech money can buy. You don't need anything high-end until you're booking enough work to justify the expense.

In the meantime, you'll want to have a quality setup that doesn't break the bank. That's probably a USB mic connected to your computer, which should be running some free audio editing software like Audacity. For a complete list of equipment, I've written a free VO resource guide, which you can find at ActingCareerMentor.com. And for a deep dive into the details, consider picking up a copy of *The Voice Over Startup Guide,* especially if you're new to VO.

Your agent will send you an email with the audition details and script. Follow the instructions. Some auditions want you to read the copy two or three times, some want you to label the file a certain way. When you're happy with your takes, you'll send an .mp3 back to your agent or upload it to a casting platform.

On the rarest of occasions, you might have a VO audition held at an outside location. In these cases, you probably won't be given the script ahead of time. You'll get it when you arrive, and leave it behind as you leave. This is how it used to be all the time, and the best voice talent were very good at performing pieces they had never seen before!

Commercial Print

Virtual photo galleries have mostly replaced in-person print auditions, though they do occasionally still happen. These auditions are called "look-sees." Your agent will send you to a photographer's studio. Casting directors sometimes work on print, but not often. You'll bring along a headshot and wear whatever the job calls for, which you'll be told ahead of time. When you get to the studio, you'll sign in and wait for your turn in front of the camera. They'll explain the shot to you and walk you through it. Once a few images are snapped, you're done. If there are a lot of people at the look-see, we call those "cattle calls" because it feels like you're just one cow in a huge herd. If you hear people mooing, that's why.

Trade Shows/Live Events

Auditions for these jobs are the most likely to happen in person, because part of the job involves seeing how you perform in front of a group of people. They are run much like auditions for industrials and happen at your agent's office, a client's office, or at some other location. Casting may handle this work, but clients will often bypass them and go directly to agents for talent.

Sometimes these auditions happen at unusual places. I've met potential clients at convention centers and hotel conference rooms. This is usually because they're in town and we meet them where they are, but I've also had self-taped auditions for live events. The deal is the same here. You'll do your prepared script, either on the ear prompter or not, and you'll be given feedback, which you should incorporate into your second take.

TV/Film

Auditions for TV and film roles run the gamut from simple one-liners to multiple scenes. Your script can be a half-page long or many pages. If they're going to happen live, these auditions are almost always held at casting director's offices.

Casting directors provide readers. The job is mostly filled by casting assistants, but sometimes they'll bring in actors to be readers. Most are pretty good, though in fairness they may be great, terrible, or somewhere in between. Readers usually try to give you a little something to work with, without taking the focus off you. You'll do a take of the scene and then be given direction. You'll incorporate the new ideas as best you can for the second take, and if they think you need a third, you'll get one. If not, you're on your way.

If it's a self-taped audition, you'll have as many takes as you need to get the scene the way you want it. However, I would suggest limiting yourself to just a few, as there is such a thing as overdoing it. Put the time into your prep instead of doing takes.

Callbacks

The organizers of many auditions plan for a second one, called a "callback." Not everyone gets to do the callback. It's reserved for the actors who seem most right for the job based on what they did in the first audition.

Callbacks can be virtual, though it's more common to have a callback in person with a virtual element. An actor would go to a casting office with a client or two in the room, but streamed to other clients in a faraway location. We might also do a callback from home via videoconference. In any case, you can expect more people to watch your callback than your first audition.

When I'm doing a virtual callback, I'm all about setting up a comfortable environment. I post the script where I can easily see it, I boost the air conditioning if need be, and I make sure to have water nearby. The great thing about auditioning from home is that we can have some ownership of the situation.

Usually we perform the same script, though once in a while we'll be sent one that's been updated. If the callback is at a casting office, there will likely be cue cards hung next to the camera. While we're not expected to be memorized for the first round of auditions, by the callback we should be pretty close to off book. This is true for just about any type of audition except for VO. Again, it's not critical to be memorized, but it'll look better if you are.

Callbacks work just like first auditions except we could be asked to do more takes with as many variations as the client would like to see. We can never read their minds, but conventional wisdom holds that more takes is a good thing. It means they're liking what we're doing, but trying to get us closer to the performance they envision. They also might be considering how well we respond to direction, or they could be looking for new ideas for the scene. Clients like versatility, so the more flexible we are, the better.

Pro tip: begin every callback by doing what you did in the first audition. You must have been on the right track if you were asked back for the second round. If they need you to adjust, they'll say so.

Check Avail

Usually there's one more hoop we have to jump through before the job is officially ours. After the callback, the field of potential candidates is narrowed even further. The next email we get might not be "you got the job," but rather "you're on check avail."

"Check avail" is short for checking your availability. It means the client has given us notice that they want first dibs on us for the scheduled shoot day. Once we agree to the job date(s), they have two choices for how to proceed. They can either book us, which means we got the job, or release us, which means someone else did.

When a short list of actors is on avail, final casting decisions are being made. Tapes are being viewed by all the clients who have casting input. That may be an ad agency creative team, a movie producer, or a network casting executive. Casting is always a team effort.

Being on check avail is a promising step, but it doesn't mean we have the job. It's common for clients to put multiple actors on avail, but only one can get the booking. I've been on avail and released a dozen times in a year. This is more common in commercials than any other work category, but there are avails for everything, including TV and film.

Once a decision has been made, only then will a call go out to the choice. If it's you, terrific, your agent will get a call with an offer for work. If it's not, your agent will get the other kind of call, the one releasing you from that date, and your journey with that particular audition has come to an end.

Tips and Tricks

There are some things we can do in any audition to help snag the job. They range from the practical to the psychological. None of them will guarantee that we'll be hired, but none of them will hurt our chances, either. Incorporating all of them into our routine will help bring a little order to our process.

First, plan ahead as much as possible. When we get our script, we need to think it through and rehearse it. If it's a commercial and the company or product is new to us, we should look it up online. Same thing if we don't know the writer or director of a film or TV show. We should watch an episode of the show or read the whole script if it's available. Look up the director and writer on IMDb and see what else they've done. Simple things like this can go a long way toward feeling prepared.

You never want to be late, if at all possible. Auditions have to be submitted on time. Once a deadline passes, we're locked out of submitting. Rushing just makes us less focused on the work.

In the audition, we try not to do anything that will call negative attention to ourselves. Even if it's a self-taped audition, never, ever go to any audition smelling of smoke, weed, or alcohol. Doing so is unprofessional. Sean Bradley, a friend of mine who owns The Green Room Studio in Chicago, tells his students that you should be relaxed and do the audition like you've had two beers, but don't *actually* have two beers before your appointment.

Last, in a callback we should wear whatever we wore the first time around. Sometimes clients remember us by our shirt color, or by something else we wore in the audition. Don't give them a reason to ask, "Where's the girl in the brown top?"

Mindset Hacks

I expect to get every job for which I audition. This puts me in a position of power, even when I'm not sure that I'm right for the role. To me, every job is mine to lose. I just have to help the decision-makers see it that way. Don't confuse this with arrogance or cockiness. I believe that approaching our auditions with a sense of accomplishment brings us a little confidence we may not otherwise have.

After any audition, it's good to allow ourselves ten minutes to think about what we did, then forget it. Actors are good at mentally replaying their auditions over and over again. Because we can always learn something from past experience, it can be beneficial to look back on what happened. Yet too much of this is pointless. Once we walk out of the room, we can't change what we did. And we really can't read minds, so we'll never be able to tell what the clients are thinking about our performance. So like the song says, let it go. This is essential to our mental health and longevity in the business.

Remember that anything can happen. We may think we have a job locked up, and not get it. We may think we performed horribly, and end up booking it. One can never tell what anyone else is thinking. Even if they express support for us in our audition, there is always the chance that someone else will overrule them. We don't know if we have a job until we're on the set or in the studio. Period.

Auditioning is a skill, and like any muscle, if we don't use it, we'll lose it. Going a few months without practice leads to rustiness. Everyone experiences gaps between auditions. To stay sharp, get into a class. If that seems impractical, practice those self-tapes. Dig up some old scripts and do them for fun. Watch your performance and honestly ask yourself if you'd hire you.

Finally, the best piece of advice I have ever heard about auditioning is this: understand that everyone wants us to do well. No one wants us to fail. In a sense, everyone in the room is auditioning for someone else. We're auditioning for the casting director, who is auditioning for the client, who is auditioning for their client, network, or studio, who is putting content out for an audience. It'll either work or it won't, but its chances improve with good actors in the project.

So even though it may feel like it's us against them, everyone in the whole process wants actors to do an amazing job every time. If we remember that we love to act, and every audition presents an opportunity to do just that, we'll be grateful for every chance we get.

Chapter Six

Working

C ongratulations, you booked the job! After the dopamine hit of getting the good news wears off, it's time to do the work. Some readers might say, "OMG, I've never done this before." Others could quietly admit, "Hallelujah, I can really use the money." Still others might shout, "I'm so glad I read Chris Agos's book!" Whatever your reaction, it'll help to know what to expect on the job.

Commercials

There can be so much variation on these jobs that it's hard to describe a "typical" scenario. Some commercial shoots last a day, some a week. They can happen locally or out of town. Their setups can be simple or very complicated. We'll go through an easy example.

You've been booked on a commercial for a large national retailer. They sell sporting goods, and you're hired as a spokesperson. You deliver the main message of the commercial by speaking your lines directly to the camera. The job shoots locally, and you've been hired for one day.

Your agent will give you the details, but the production company may also reach out to you. It's common to get a call from the wardrobe department, who will want to check your sizes to make sure they're providing you with clothes that fit well and look good on camera. They may also ask you to bring a few of your own things.

You'll eventually get your final script, but it may not come until the night before the shoot. Scripts are often updated and not distributed until the ad agency knows it's final. However, "final" scripts can also be updated, sometimes as you're shooting them. Just stay flexible.

Shoot days are meticulously planned, so it's important that you arrive on time. Schedules are set well in advance, and there's little room for error. Specifically, the production company doesn't want the cast and crew to go into overtime. This usually happens when everyone's been there for more than nine or ten hours, after which they're paid time and a half. Often this can't be helped, but don't let it be your fault.

Let's assume you've arrived at the location, one of the client's stores, on time. When you walk in, someone will tell you where to park yourself and your stuff. Your first stop will probably be wardrobe. If they asked you to bring some of your own clothes, they'll want to see them. Before making a final decision on what you'll wear in the spot, they may have you try on some options. Then you'll head to makeup, which likely won't be with the same person. Plan on arriving with your face clean unless you're told otherwise.

There will also be someone there to do your hair. You might wonder what kind of style you should go with. There's no hard rule. Some producers will tell you to show up with your hair completely unstyled so the on-set stylist can do whatever they need to with it. More often we're asked to arrive looking like it did at the audition or callback. Don't cut, straighten, color, or otherwise alter your hair between the callback and the shoot unless you're asked to do so. Guys should not alter facial hair. If you're just not sure what to do, ask your agent.

When you're dressed and made up, you'll want to be careful with your look. The stylists will be watching you like hawks to make sure you don't wrinkle your clothes or mess up your hair. Just be mindful of your actions during any downtime.

You'll eventually be brought to the set by a production assistant or some other crew member. They've got another job besides babysitting you, but they'll be your point of contact for the day. If you've got questions or concerns, they're the one to ask. On some jobs you won't have this kind of person, but usually someone makes it known that you're to come to them if you need anything.

On your way to set, or perhaps when you get there, someone from the sound department will likely need to mic you. This involves securing a microphone somewhere near your collar and running the wires inside your shirt down to a transmitter, which you'll wear on your waist or at your ankle. It's about the size of a small deck of cards and must be hidden. You'll be asked to say a few words for a sound check. Pro tip: running through your script attracts unwanted attention. Instead, count backward from ten.

Once on set, you'll be shown your start mark and end mark for the day's first shot. They're referred to with numbers. The start mark is your "one," and your end mark is your "two." When someone says, "Go back to one," they want you back on your start mark. These marks will change with different shots.

Let's say you have to do some walking and talking. You'll begin on your start mark and say your lines as you move to your end mark. It's important to hit them on every take. The lighting and camera focus will be set to look their best between these two points. Not only that, but your pacing will have to be accurate. You may need to adjust how quickly you walk if they want you to get all your lines in between your one and two.

You'll have a few chances to rehearse the move, then it'll be time to start doing takes. The set will get very quiet. Everyone will have done their jobs, and the focus will now be on you. Sound will be listening for mic rustles in your clothing, makeup will be looking for sheen on your face, hair will be looking for flyaways. Wardrobe will be looking for weirdness with your clothing. Props will be looking at the racks of sports equipment, so at least you don't have their attention. This moment can be tense for actors because of the scrutiny.

The director will be in charge from this point forward. This might be the first time they share some of their thoughts with you about what they're looking for in your performance. I've had conversations that have run the gamut from, "Do what you did in your callback," to "The client wants something totally new." Expect the unexpected and be willing to take direction.

When shooting begins, you'll do take after take. An assistant director may call action or cut, but it's the director who will pass you feedback from the client as the shoot progresses. You'll likely be asked to vary your delivery from take to take.

When they're happy with the takes they have, they'll go again by pushing in for closeups or grabbing other camera angles. You might do the script a hundred times. This is normal and doesn't mean you're doing a terrible job!

Eventually, you'll work through the day's shot list and when you're done, you'll be released from set. You'll change out of wardrobe (remember to hang it up), clean your face, gather your things, and thank everyone for the work. Then you're on your way home.

As you book more spots, you'll discover that some shoots are handled more elaborately than others. You could encounter crews of just a few people, or large ones where even the wardrobe stylist has an assistant or two. There's really no way to predict what you'll run into. Common to all jobs is actor downtime. We do a lot of waiting, so bring a book. Honestly, it's a great way to kill time.

Industrials

This is another broad category of work that can have a ton of variation. You can be the only actor on the set or part of a large cast. There are jobs that will require very little work on your part, and ones where you'll have the most responsibility. Some shoots will be complicated, others as simple as can be.

Generally, there are two types of industrial jobs: narration and role-playing. In on-camera narration, an actor delivers a script while looking directly into the camera as if he's speaking to the audience on the other side of it. Role-playing jobs, also called "day player jobs," feature two or more actors playing out a scene while ignoring the camera, like what you see in a movie or a play.

Shoot locations are often owned or occupied by the company for which you're working. These can vary widely. You might shoot in a factory or a science lab. Industrials are interesting because of the opportunity to learn something new. How else would you ever learn the process behind making paint, or how to change the bulb in an x-ray machine?

There's really no "typical" industrial, but most shoots last one or two days. Often, jobs scheduled for one day wind up going into overtime, because it's cheaper for clients to pay everyone a little extra than to bring them back for a second day.

We're typically asked to bring wardrobe choices to these jobs, so it helps to have a good selection of business casual clothing and at least one suit. Guys should have khakis, dress shirts, and nice polos, and women should have the same and maybe a skirt and a decent selection of accessories. We don't have to bring our whole closet, but we should have a few things ready to go. Remember to avoid anything with logos, graphics, or bold prints. Sometimes the client will provide us with certain wardrobe items, like a shirt bearing the company's logo.

Tighter budgets have mostly eliminated makeup and hair stylists from a lot of industrials, so we should be prepared to do our own. Women should ask producers what kind of look would be the most appropriate and be prepared to show up camera ready. Guys might want to keep some powder on hand to knock down any shine.

After the job, you should try to get a copy of the finished product. This goes for every type of work, actually. It can be easier said than done since companies don't like to let their content out into the wild, but that doesn't mean we can't ask for a file.

Keeping copies of everything you do can be important so you can string together clips for a reel. If you don't know what a reel looks like, have a look at mine at chrisagos.com. Reels are a minute's worth of tape showcasing some of our best work in a certain category. Actors have reels for TV/film, commercials, industrials, etc. Essentially, they're part of our marketing.

Voice Over

Every VO job happens in a recording studio of some kind. It can be in a large professional studio, or in your (possibly more modest) home recording space. Voice work is great if you can get it because the jobs are typically short, lasting anywhere from thirty minutes to a few hours. You don't have to look good or worry about wardrobe because no one cares what you look like, only what you sound like. And you can make as much money (or more) as an on-camera job while putting in a fraction of the time.

There are many kinds of VO work. I cover all of them in *The Voice Over Startup Guide*, and most can be done from home studios. Regardless of the type of work for which we're hired, the process is similar.

Let's say you're hired to voice a commercial. If you're unable to produce broadcast-quality audio at home, you'll be sent to a recording studio. As stated previously, though, it's more likely you'll be asked to record using your own equipment.

If you are heading to an outside studio, you'll check in with the receptionist. They'll let the sound engineer know you're there, and you may have to wait while they get things ready for you. You may or may not be given scripts to look at while you're waiting. If you are, quietly read them out loud to discover any words or phrases that might make you stumble. Everyone has a few words that trip them up. For the longest time I got hung up on the word "cellular." I had to quickly find a way to get over it when I became the voice of a big wireless provider.

If your session is at home, scripts will arrive via email. Prep them however you like. I shared my process in my book, *Commercial Voice Over Strategies*, so check it out if you're curious. At the time of the session, you'll connect to the client in whatever way they choose. That could be over conferencing software, or you might connect via specific VO connection software.

Recording sessions run in similar ways to commercial shoots. You'll do a practice take to set volume levels and make sure your equipment is working properly. Then you'll start doing takes, making adjustments as you're asked to do so. There should be one person giving you direction, but there could be more than that. The engineer may also have some input. When you're done, don't forget to ask the producer for a copy of the finished product. If the answer is yes, they'll likely send it after it airs.

Commercial Print

In its most basic form, a print job requires an actor to be in front of a camera for a little while and then go home. There are jobs that require more, of course, but many are just that simple. Don't let that make you think it's easy.

As always, you'll receive details prior to the job. You may be asked to confirm your clothing sizes because in most print jobs, garments that fit well are as important as the actor who acts well.

When you arrive at the photographer's studio, you'll meet the staff and be shown to a dressing area, where you'll lay out your wardrobe choices if you were asked to bring any. You'll also find any clothing they have for you. At some point you'll meet the clients, who will want to see you in wardrobe. Shots will be taken of each outfit, and the stills might be sent to someone off-site for final approval. After the final outfit choice is made, you'll be off to makeup and hair.

Print jobs are all about how you look, so there's much more scrutiny of your physical appearance than in other kinds of work. You'll be told to shift your weight, stand up straight, tilt your head one way (then another), lift your right pinky finger, rotate your left hand, and try a variety of facial expressions. This is just the tip of the iceberg. Traditionally the photographer acts as the director, but input can come from many people. Do your best to keep up with all their suggestions.

It can be tricky to get a copy of the finished product. If you're able to spot the image in the wild, hang onto it. These are called "tear sheets" because they are torn from publications, mailers, product packaging, and other physical objects. You could also take a screenshot if you see it online. You can ask for a file, but the client may be reluctant to share them.

Trade Shows/Live Events

As you read earlier, actors are hired to work a trade show as a host, crowd gatherer, product specialist, or presenter. We could also be hired as a combination of all four.

Unless we live near a show's home city, we typically have to travel for this kind of work. Big conventions are held in Las Vegas, Orlando, and New York, among other locations. It's also possible to work outside of the country in English-speaking markets. Travel expenses are usually covered by the client.

We may be hired to do a single show, but there are several companies that do multiple shows in a year. They like to hire teams of actors to travel a show circuit, heading to each city as the year progresses. When you audition you'll be told how many shows the company is looking to do.

Let's say you're booked on a single show for a company that does one show per year, and they've hired you as a presenter. Your speech, which is eight minutes long, happens every half hour. You get an hour off for lunch.

You can expect the job to start with a rehearsal day, during which any kinks will be worked out of the staging, lighting, blocking, and video elements. You'll also learn where your area is to hang out when you're not presenting, and you'll become generally familiar with the main messaging of the client. Show attendees think spokespeople work for the company, so it's good to know how to answer a few basic questions.

The morning of the first day, your call time will be very early. Clients often like to do one last rehearsal before the show floor opens. The company's employees will likely be gathered around to hear you do your thing. If it's not perfect, tweaks will be made.

Trade shows are hard work. We're on our feet all day and there can be little downtime. There may be nowhere for you to hang out between presentations, and show floors can be loud and overstimulating.

In our fictional example, you're a presenter. That means you have a script to deliver. You can memorize it or use an ear prompter. Some clients ask their presenters to use prompters because it allows them to make last-minute changes easily. Others prefer memorization. You'll be told ahead of time which they prefer.

Actors who are hired as hosts or crowd gatherers will have an orientation on the rehearsal day or very early on the morning of the first day of the show. Product specialists will likely have additional training sessions before the show to get familiar with the details of the products.

TV/Film

There's nothing quite like getting the call that you're the choice for a role in a film or TV show. It's a special feeling. Unfortunately, doing the job is usually not as exciting as finding out that you got the job.

I haven't mentioned this yet, but I have a YouTube channel. It's filled with helpful content for actors, but one of the most popular is a series of videos called *First Time Acting on TV*. It goes through every detail of what it's like to work on a TV show, step by step. Check it out when you can.

Working on a big-budget film or TV set is an exercise in waiting. Let's say you booked a role as a bartender, and they'll need you for one day. Prior to the shoot, there's almost always a phone call or two from the production folks. You'll also be emailed a call sheet, a document that organizes all the information for the day's agenda.

You can expect your call time to be very early in the morning. When you arrive, you'll be introduced to a member of the assistant director (AD) staff. It will be important for that person to know where you are at all times because they'll be responsible for getting you wherever you're supposed to be.

The first place you'll go is to your holding area, either a green room or trailer. You could be there a very, very long time. Hours, in fact, without any contact from your handler, who might be busy with other tasks. You'll likely be given an updated call sheet. In addition to the schedule of scenes being shot, it will have other information like the weather forecast, the crew roster, and a list of special equipment needed to shoot the day's scenes.

Along with the call sheet you'll be given your sides, which are the scheduled script pages for the day. Look through them because the script may have changed since you last saw it. You're usually emailed updates beforehand, but if the changes are recent enough, you might find out about them by looking at the sides. Sometimes they give you more lines, or they may take some away. Be ready for either.

Let's say your call time is 7:00 a.m. and you arrive on time. A look at the call sheet reveals you're in the third scene of the day, which means it'll be a while before they're ready for you. In that time you'll do hair and makeup, and try to stay sharp while waiting. Pro tip: don't change into your wardrobe until you're told to do so. You don't want to unnecessarily wrinkle the costume.

Eventually you'll be walked to set, which in our example is a bar. Once there, you'll be in the hands of the first assistant director (first AD) and the director, who will want to do a read through of the scene. You'll meet the other actors if you haven't been introduced already. After the read through, there will be a blocking rehearsal, which is as much for the lighting and sound departments as it is for the cast. When everyone's ready, work will begin.

Shooting will go just like any commercial or industrial. They'll do multiple takes, stopping between each to adjust as needed. Listen to the director and change your performance up as much as they ask. When the scene has been covered all the ways the director envisioned it, you're all finished. You'll say your goodbyes, be walked back to your trailer, and change out of your costume. Please hang it up. We don't want the costume department to think actors are slobs. If you'd like to remove your makeup before you leave, sometimes the stylists have hot towels or removal wipes.

Adjust your expectations when you're working on projects with smaller budgets. There may be fewer crew members on set. You may have to do your own hair or makeup. There might not even be a call sheet if you're working with a very small and informal indie film production. If everyone's working for free, you'll be asked to bring your own wardrobe and maybe a prop or two. There are productions up and down the spectrum, and when you audition for something, you'll know what kind you're dealing with.

The working conditions you're likely to run into while shooting TV and film depend largely on whether you're working on a union set. All scripted large-budget Hollywood-based productions are union, as are many smaller independent films. We'll learn more about the union in a later chapter.

About AI

In 2023, artificial intelligence exploded into the public consciousness. In creative fields like ours, it introduced a whole new set of worries, what-if scenarios, and concerns about how this new generative technology could potentially replace the humans who make movies and TV shows.

For emerging actors, the question is, "Will this AI thing prevent me from becoming an actor?" The answer is no, it will not stand in the way of anyone looking to launch an acting career, nor will it stop them from making good progress toward a goal. A lot of the angst around AI comes from the unknowns about the future. The technology is so new that no one really knows where it's going to take us, how it's going to be used, or what its impact will be on the industry.

Hollywood has been using visual effects and computer generated images (VFX and CGI) for decades. AI is just another form of those things, except this new tech makes it possible to create, store, and re-use digital doubles of actors. This is done through the use of a process commonly called "scanning," where still images of an actor are stitched together to make a three dimensional representation of that actor. Because it's made up of data, this new synthetic performer can be altered in any way imaginable, and placed into any project.

Currently, the process of scanning, storing, and manipulating these synthetic performers is exceedingly complicated and expensive, so much so that producers and visual effects artists prefer to do things the old-fashioned way: by using a camera to capture the performances of real human actors on a set. When a performer's scan is going to be used, the producer has to notify the performer, get their permission to use the scan, and pay the actor for the time their digital replica is in use. This means that AI could potentially have benefits for actors as they gain the option to "rent out" their digital doubles on days when they're physically shooting a different project.

The point is that AI isn't something a new actor should be worrying much about. My advice is to keep an eye on its development, but don't let it live rent-free in your mind. There are far more important things to think about as you launch your career.

Action Items

Things you can do right now:

- Familiarize yourself with work categories that are new to you. VO? Print?

- Check YouTube, Vimeo, and other sources for examples of industrials or trade show presentations.

- Begin researching local actor training facilities and read online reviews.

- Do the same for online programs.

- Look up some acting coaches. Read about them and listen to what they have to say.

- Decide which area of the business you want to learn first.

- Research commercial photographers in your local area.

- Resolve to listen to every commercial on TV, all the way through.

- Make a list of barriers to starting. Brainstorm solutions because everything is fixable.

- Subscribe to one or more acting podcasts.

- Think about which work categories seem the most doable for you right now. Commercials? VO?

- Follow trade publications on social media: Adweek, Deadline Hollywood, Variety, etc.

- Begin plotting changes to your work life to accommodate for daytime availability.

- Jot down some short-term goals and ones for the longer term.

- Start connecting with other actors online.

- Go see some local theatrical productions. Sometimes there

are Q&A sessions after the show. Attend them. Ask questions.

- Begin looking up various acting techniques. Is there one that
  speaks to you more than the others?

- What do you think your type is as an actor? Why?

Part 2

The Tools

Chapter Seven

Headshots

A ctors have a job to do, and we need tools to do it. When it comes to on-camera work, the three most important are a headshot, an online casting profile, and a self-tape setup. These things are our lifeline to whatever we want out of this business.

Even if you're new to the profession, you've probably seen examples of professional headshots. They're usually the first way an actor introduces themselves to the industry, which makes them significant.

The most important thing about our headshot is that it looks like us. It should not look like the person we hope to be some day, or the person that we really wish we were, but the one that we are right now.

While it's fine to dress up nicely, put on some makeup, and have multiple headshots to reflect different moods (maybe one for comedy, another for drama), we never want to stray too far from who we really are. When a dark and mysterious-looking thirtysomething submits a headshot that makes them look like a bright, bubbly twenty-year-old, that actor is misrepresenting themselves. If casting needs a bubbly twentysomething for their job, they'll be very disappointed when they get someone who looks ten years older in real life. We want to start a new relationship on the right foot, so accuracy counts.

Our headshots should not only look like us, but also be compelling. They should tell a story about what we bring to the party. It's not enough to sit in front of the camera and smile pretty. That's what our kids do at the beginning of every school year. Those pictures are a nice record of what kids look like over time, but no one ever considers them and says, "I could see her in a single-cam dramedy."

We begin building an effective headshot by having an idea about how we want the industry to see us. Our styling, lighting, background, and shot angle will combine to deliver the intended message.

Your Photographer

Who we choose to help us with headshots will have a great impact on the result. If you're wondering whether it's worth spending the money on a professional headshot photographer, let me assure you that it is. Even if acting is just a side gig, you absolutely cannot get away with cutting corners on your headshot. There are lots of reasons why that is, but the biggest issue is credibility. Actors have to look like we know what we're doing, even if we don't know anything at all. A well-crafted headshot will hold up against all the others. We want to give ourselves the best chance to succeed, so we hire experienced professionals when necessary.

Photographers are available almost anywhere in the US, yet I would encourage you to be selective. Experience counts, so choose one who has worked with actors. Someone who mostly shoots weddings and family portraits may be excellent in those settings, but may not be familiar with the requirements of our industry. Have a look at plenty of online galleries before you decide who to hire, and if your best choice is a couple hours' drive away, don't hesitate to hop in the car.

When you find someone you're excited about, don't hire them right away. Most photographers offer free no-obligation consultations. These appointments may happen in person or virtually, but it's important to do them either way. You have to know that you'll be comfortable with the photographer. We want to sit for someone we could hang out with. In contrast, if we run into someone who makes us a little nervous, or who seems disorganized and aloof, that's going to show up in our shots.

If your initial appointment is in person, hopefully you're meeting at their studio. Look around and note the general feel of the place. Do you get good vibes? Were you greeted with a pleasant smile when you arrived? Do they make you feel welcome? Do you sense an air of brisk activity or stifled boredom?

While you're at it, were you able to find parking? Can you play your own music during the shoot? Use the bathroom while you're there, or check out the dressing room if there is one. Are they clean and bright? All these elements will come together for you on the day of your shoot, and any of them could affect how you feel, and thus influence the result of your shots.

A lot of photographers don't have studios. There are plenty who instead use various locations as backdrops for their photos and touch up the images at home. They may schedule your consultation virtually. With appointments like these, it's less about where you're going to be shooting (although that's definitely a question you should be asking) and more about their policies. Ask about deposits, package pricing, turnaround times, and editing costs. Some photographers include a certain number of finished images with the price of the session, and others don't.

You'll likely be offered different options when it comes to looks. You can think of a look like a mood change, where you'd use a different background, clothing, or hairstyle to convey different ideas. A good example of this is a smiley headshot, which is commonly used for commercial auditions, compared to a more serious headshot, which might be used for TV/film. More looks usually mean a higher price for the session.

While all these things are good to take stock of, the most important factor in choosing a shooter is how easily you interact with them. More than anything, you want to feel comfortable in front of their lens.

The Shoot

Once you've chosen a photographer, you'll have to schedule your shoot. Think about this a little, and know that it's not just a matter of when you and the photographer are both available. Consider what time of day you look and feel your best. Some people are early risers, while some are night owls.

When selecting a date, try to make sure you have nothing else to do that day. The idea is to keep the day as stress-free as possible, and you don't want to be under any time pressure. Try to pick a time when you know your schedule will be predictable and relaxed.

There are photographers who will go out of their way to make sure you get the best shots possible. These are the professionals who make the sessions all about the actor, not about the photographer. They're the ones who ask you what you want, and give it to you. You want to look like a vixen from the 1940s? You got it. You need to seem tough and dirty, yet sensitive and educated? No problem. The good ones know that your livelihood depends on the end result. If you find a photographer who does this, keep them in your contact list. Avoid those who are pushy and believe their way is the only way. Headshots are a collaborative effort.

Policies and procedures differ, but after your session is finished, you can expect that every usable frame taken will be posted to an online gallery. You might have hundreds of images to go through. Get comfortable in front of your computer and take a good look at all of them. Mark your favorites. Remember, you're looking for shots that best express who you are.

Outside opinions can be valuable. Get a teacher, another actor, or better yet an agent if you have one, to give you their honest opinion about which shot or shots seem like winners. I'm not a fan of posting them to your socials because you might get some unreliable feedback. Most of your followers probably don't know much about what makes an actor's headshot effective.

A word of warning: family members (especially mothers) will usually love any headshot of you and thus aren't good sources for unbiased opinions. You want to have someone with a critical eye look at your shots. Your photographer might be one person you could ask for input.

It will hopefully be difficult to narrow the shots down to just one choice from each look, but that's your goal. When you inform the photographer of your final picks, they'll likely do some post-processing on them, cleaning up things like skin blemishes and flyaway hairs. Sometimes this service is included in the price, but other times it's not, so ask beforehand. Then you'll be sent the files. Often there will be several file types and sizes. You'll have files for printing, web-size ones for posting, and sometimes files with specs that are ideal for certain online casting platforms.

There are differing opinions about whether actors still need physical headshots printed on 8x10 paper. Most casting happens online now, nearly eliminating the need for physical prints. Yet in certain circumstances, we are still asked for them. Consider picking your favorite shot and getting a handful of prints duplicated. Go with fifty. It's better to have them and not need them, than the other way around. I use a duplication house in Los Angeles called Argentum Studios. They can do everything by mail, they're affordable, and they do great work. If there isn't a photo duplication facility near you, look them up.

Geography has a lot to do with pricing, but plan on spending somewhere between $300 and $700 before your headshots are ready to be seen by the industry. That may not include extras like hiring a hair and makeup stylist ($75–$150), paying the photographer a little extra to travel to a shoot location ($100–$250), additional image files ($10–$25 each), retouching your images ($25–$100 each image), or buying clothes specifically for your shoot (sky's the limit).

A good headshot is an investment in ourselves. It's a tool an actor can't live without, and the right one pays dividends for years.

Chapter Eight

Resumes and Casting Profiles

W e've got a great headshot, and now we need to tell people what we're up to. For that we use resumes combined with profiles at casting websites. Your headshot makes the first impression, but your resume and profile can help seal the deal.

Actors typically have three versions of their resume: a physical version, a digital copy in the form of a PDF, and a resume that is part of their actor profiles. The same rules apply to all of them, with the exception of formatting. Some casting sites handle that for us, but we'll need to format the other resume types. Because of that, let's talk about best practices for building a good resume.

A resume will always accompany a headshot. When we use physical resumes, they are printed on a piece of paper that's trimmed to the size of our 8x10 headshot. I bring a stack of plain white printer paper somewhere like FedEx Office and have them use their flat cutter to trim the whole stack down to 8x10. Then, using my printer at home,

I print resumes as I need them. I staple the resume to my headshot back-to-back so the viewer can look at the image on one side and flip it over to reveal the resume on the other side. Two staples at the top take care of it. The idea is to make the whole thing look clean and professional. Most of us won't need them often, but when we are asked for them, it's good to present them correctly.

To create the digital version of our well-crafted physical resume, simply save or export the file as a PDF. You'll email this PDF to potential industry partners like agents and managers. More on these folks later.

Casting directors in the US and Canada use a handful of websites to organize and send out their auditions. It's imperative that every actor have profiles at these sites. With no profile, there's no chance of being given the chance to audition, especially for film and TV work. We all sign up for at least a basic membership at each of these sites. They are generally free, but some fees do apply. You might already know which sites I'm referring to, but we'll talk more about them in a bit.

The terminology is a little tricky since sites use the words "resume" and "profile" interchangeably. I'll use them the same way, but just know that both refer to the document you put together to show others in the industry who you are and what you've been up to.

Let's start with the information you should include, how to organize it, and what can be left out.

Building a Resume and Profile

Headshots are the attention getters, but resumes are the substance, so we've got to give them something honest, organized, and compelling. Actors with training and work behind them can skip the next paragraph. This one's for those with no experience at all.

No one's born with a fantastic resume, and everyone has to start their professional acting career from scratch. That's expected by the industry. If you're just beginning, you've probably taken at least one class (acting, improv, dance, voice, etc.) or been in some kind of production (school, community theater, children's theater, etc.). These count as resume items. The question you have to ask about each one is this: Does it directly and obviously relate to the kind of work you're now going after? If the answer is honestly no (like emceeing a nonprofit's fund raiser), then leave it off. It's better to have few to no real credits than a resume filled with irrelevant items. If you've got nothing to list, get into an acting class. I don't care what kind, just take one that excites you.

And if you're tempted to make something up, don't. It'll come back to bite you in the worst way, and you won't recover from it. Would you really want your career sunk before it even starts?

An Example

Let's look at a sample resume, one that would be printed and stapled to the back of a physical headshot. Though most resumes appear as attachments to online casting profiles, this format allows us to easily see their nuances.

Andrew Actor
SAG-AFTRA
Sample Talent Agency, Inc.
samplewebaddress.tv

| Height: 5'10" Weight: 165 | Eyes: Brown | Hair: Blond | Suit: 40R |

Film
Feature Length Movie #2	Lead	Director Name/Studio Name
Feature Length Movie #2	Supporting	Director Name/Studio Name
Feature Length Movie #3	Supporting	Director Name/Studio Name

TV
TV Series #1	Recurring	Director Name/Network Name
TV Series #2	Recurring	Director Name/Network Name
TV Series #3	Recurring	Director Name/Network Name
TV Series #4	Guest Star	Director Name/Network Name
TV Series #5	Guest Star	Director Name/Network Name
TV Series #6	Costar	Director Name/Network Name
TV Series #7	Costar	Director Name/Network Name

Theater
Production Title #1	Character Name	Director/Theater Name
Production Title #2	Character Name	Director/Theater Name
Production Title #3	Character Name	Director/Theater Name
Production Title #4	Character Name	Director/Theater Name

Commercials
Ad Agency #1, Ad Agency #2, Ad Agency #3, or "Conflict list available upon request."

Industrials
Company #1	Company #2	Company #3	Company #4

Trade Shows
Company #1	Company #2	Company #3	Company #4

Education/Training
Undergrad/Grad Degree	Institution Name	Discipline (Theatre, Psych, etc.)
Class #1	Institution Name	Instructor Name
Class #2	Institution Name	Instructor Name
Coach #1	Discipline (voice, scene study, dialects, etc.)	

Special Skills/Interests
Skill #1, Skill #2, Skill #3, etc.

An acting resume is divided into sections. In the header is the actor's name, union status, and personal information. Our union status lets people know which auditions we can do. We'll learn more about unions later, but if you're not a member, leave this blank. Don't write "Nonunion" or "Pre-union."

Our contact information should not include a physical address or phone number. An email or website works better; however, any website listed should be devoted to our acting work. If our site showcases our abilities in something else, like a previous career, visitors will wonder why we sent them there.

Physical stats are included because sometimes we're cast with others who are shorter or taller than we are, and it makes a difference to the casting folks. This section also gives viewers an idea of our physical stature. Men should list their suit size, and women their dress size.

Below the header is the actor's work experience. We list credits by work category, following the "impressive first" strategy. We want to highlight the most competitive, most watched, or most interesting work we've done. For a lot of actors, that means listing film and TV credits first. However, some talent may choose to lead with other credit types, especially if they've done a lot of stage work. Actors who haven't yet done TV, film, or stage work can lead off with any category of work they've done.

We also want to follow this strategy within categories. For example, if we've done a lot of very small roles in TV shows but have one larger role under our belt, we'll lead with that one even if it's older than the rest.

You'll notice that most work categories have a three-column format, which makes everything easier to absorb at a glance. Each category requires different information. With TV, we list the name of the show, the type of role for which we were hired, the director, and network or streamer on which it ran. Same with film, except we list the director and movie studio. Some markets, like New York, use four columns. The director's name would occupy the third, and the network or studio would be listed fourth.

Our strategy can be extended to the industrial and trade show categories, but there's hardly a project that will be recognizable to anyone not working in those areas. Once an actor has a lot of these credits, they can just name the company they worked for, or list the names of the trade shows they've done.

There are so many types of VO work that it can be difficult to know how to list any of them. Some actors choose to leave VO off their resumes. It's definitely legitimate acting work, and in certain markets it can count for a lot, so I will always recommend listing it if it's something the actor is actively pursuing. Commercial and video game VO might be very recognizable to readers, so if an actor has those credits, they'd lead with them. Audiobook narration and TV series narration might also be beneficial. What to list here depends on where the actor is based, and the opinion of the actor's representatives, which we'll learn more about later.

Print can be left off an acting resume; however, if an actor is also a model, it's possible to make a statement about the work they've done instead of listing individual credits. This can include something similar to what we do with commercials.

Speaking of, you'll notice that the commercials category is different from all the others. We would never list the products or brand names we're helping to advertise. This is because of product conflicts. The details vary, but advertisers generally don't want to hire actors who have worked for competing brands.

Let's say your first commercial was for an automaker. You did it years ago, and it's no longer running. You're submitted to audition for another car commercial, this one for a different brand. Problem is, your submission is passed over. You fit the requirements for the role, but the casting director declines to audition you because your resume reveals that you've worked for a competing manufacturer.

Is this fair? Well, it doesn't really matter. Casting works very quickly, and they are not going to take the time to find out that your commercial hasn't run in years. They know that an automaker isn't going to want an actor promoting their product while also working with a competitor. They'll just move on to other actors who also fit the role's requirements.

To get around this, we have two choices. One is to list the names of advertising agencies on our resume in place of the brand names. This is an option if we'd like to tell the world how many commercials we've done. Those in the ad industry will see that we've been cast across multiple agencies, making us look more castable.

The other option is to list the phrase "Conflict list available upon request," under the commercials category. This implies that we *might* have a product conflict, yet it's very noncommittal. What I love about this statement is that it gives the impression that we could have some commercial experience, yet if we don't and we're asked about it, we'll be truthful and answer that we don't have any current conflicts.

The education category might be where all the action is when an actor is new to the business. Here we'll list our industry training, along with any education that might be interesting or beneficial to readers. We can list our undergraduate and graduate degrees even if they're not in theater. We can also list any interesting certifications.

If an actor is a first responder, or member of the military, those are potentially valuable to a casting director and should be included. Obviously, our acting training should be given priority.

We list items in this category in a visually pleasing way. There's no hard rule about the number of columns. What should be listed is the name of the training center, or in the case of private coaching, the name of the person with whom the actor trained.

Finally, the special skills section is where you get to have some fun. There's no format to follow other than to make it a short list of things you do well. This is a chance to tell people who you really are, however briefly. Whatever you're good at, include it here. If you're big into martial arts, put it down. If you're a fire eater, list it. If you've swum the English Channel or hold the world record for cramming the highest number of packing peanuts up your nose, make darn sure that's on there. The more unique and memorable the skill, the better.

You should only include stuff you can actually do. If you ski, but only on the bunny hill and you fall face first every other run, you don't really ski. At least you probably couldn't do it take after take. Get the work you should be getting.

Leave the Background

Many actors do background work as a way of staying busy between larger acting jobs. This is fine, but not resume worthy. Background players (also known as extras) work hard for not a lot of pay. The job can be difficult and sometimes occupies a lot of an actor's time. It's no wonder some actors think it should be included it on resumes.

But it shouldn't, and the reason is that resumes are for roles that actors have gotten through an audition process. There is none for background players. I'm not saying actors shouldn't do this work. It's a great way to get on set and can be a fantastic education, but it should be left off a professional resume.

Other Considerations

Every acting market has its own quirks. You may find that resumes in your area are formatted a little differently than what's described here. Complicating things are talent representatives who may have an opinion about how an actor's resume should be written.

That's all fine, and good to know. Don't be afraid to make changes or include work categories that aren't mentioned here. For example, actors coming from the improv world could include that experience on their resumes. Same for singers and dancers looking to move into acting. If it's related to performance, it might be worth including. Just remember that if it's unrelated to the type of work you're going after, it should be left out.

Online Casting Profiles

There are currently three main casting sites used by the industry to find and cast professional actors: actorsaccess.com, castingnetwor ks.com, and castingfrontier.com. At first glance it might seem like their primary purpose is to allow actors to submit themselves for paying roles. That's part of their function, but the industry does not necessarily use them in that way. Instead, casting directors organize and run their auditions with them, agents use them to submit their talent, and actors use them to be available for and sometimes execute auditions.

Actors can also submit themselves for projects, but that usually involves a paid membership. Basic memberships are generally free with agent representation. I'll let each site give you membership details since they're all a little different. The most dominant site at the time of this writing is probably actorsaccess.com. A look around the site can explain things better than I can here, but if you've never used it before, let's cover some basics.

Actors register for and maintain accounts and profiles on the site. We'll upload headshots and use their resume builder, a tool that lays out resumes for the industry to view. Having a resume already formatted for print will make the process very easy. We choose our work categories and layout in addition to entering all our work information. If we have an agent, we'll tell the site who they are so they can include us in the agency's roster. The agent will have to confirm that we are, in fact, represented by their agency.

When a casting director posts a project and our agent thinks we may be right for it, they'll submit our profile. The casting office will gather all the submissions, look at each one, and mark the actors they want to see. If we're on that list, our agent will be notified and will send us the casting notice. It'll have all the details about the audition and the job. We'll have to confirm or decline the audition and if we accept, then we'll follow the directions given.

Getting the most out of these sites starts with having the correct notification settings. If we don't know about an audition, we're going to miss it. The sites allow us to customize how we receive notifications. I recommend getting them by text and email.

The other important thing about our profiles is that we have to keep them current. They are front-facing to the industry and can't be left to die on the vine. We upload new headshots when they're taken, update our resumes, and post video clips when we have them. We also keep our size cards updated if they change. This is because casting will likely give production staff access to our information when we book a job. The size card will go to the wardrobe stylist, who may be buying clothes for us. If they buy the wrong sizes, we will make them mad. Never make a stylist mad. They're in charge of making us look good!

Chapter Nine

Self-Taping Setups

O nce we're selected to audition, it's likely we'll be taping that audition ourselves. The process is fairly straightforward but requires a having a bit of gear. You probably have some of it already, and the rest can be picked up relatively inexpensively.

Our self-taping system should be affordable, reliable, and repeatable. We want to keep the mysteries to a minimum, especially if we have to tape something on short notice. Instead of reinventing the wheel every time we have an audition, developing some muscle memory around our routine will allow us to know exactly what to do every time we do it.

In any audition, our very first obligation is to do justice to the script we're given. The shift to self-taping means our second job is to produce an audition that will hold up next to the others that will be submitted. To accomplish this, we'll need to focus on three things: the look, the sound, and the file.

The Look

The visuals of any self-taped audition should be completely focused on you. That means the viewer should be able to see you clearly and not be distracted by (or forced to look at) anything else in the shot.

In a perfect world, everyone would have about eight uninterrupted feet of plain wall, and do all their self-tapes in front of it. In this world, you'd be able to paint the wall any color, it would be free from blemishes like cracks and picture hooks, and it would be in a quiet place with nice, even lighting. Most of us don't have a space like that, so there are a few different ways to create one.

One option is to hang a sheet against a wall. This will work as long as it isn't wrinkled and doesn't have any weird impressions coming from stuff hanging on the wall. You don't want to tape in front of something that looks like Han Solo encased in carbonite. Pro tip: make sure to anchor the bottom corners so it doesn't float around as you move in the scene.

A step up involves using a large piece of foam core as a backdrop. It's like really thick poster board and is sold in various sizes at craft and photography stores. Get the biggest one they have, which will probably be just large enough to do closeup shots. You can order larger sizes if you want the option to shoot wider. When it arrives, you'll need to hang it. Some actors tape it up, others punch holes in the foam core and hang it on nails, still others use a stand with a clamp attachment made to hold flat objects. Any of these is fine as long as the hardware is mostly out of the shot. The downside to foam core is that it's not durable. It gets marked up and damaged pretty easily. It's also hard to store because it's rigid, so it doesn't fold.

Most actors eventually invest in a portable backdrop. Some are collapsible, some are two-sided with dark and light options, and some are solid rolls of paper or fabric that can roll out of the way when you're not using them. Sizes range from 4x4 squares of fabric to 8x13 rolls of paper.

Whatever backdrop you choose, it should be a single color, or a very soft wash of similar colors. There isn't one "right" color. Some casting offices tell you they prefer a blue background, others say they like a light gray. Stay away from dark colors, which are tricky to light. I'd also avoid stark white backgrounds. You can't go wrong with a light blue or gray. Avoid chroma key green, which is not flattering, and skip the metallic reflector. You don't want anything shiny or reflective in your background.

The shot should be fully and evenly lit. The simplest and least expensive option for lighting is the sun. If you have a large window, it can be your primary light source. Some people face a window and put the back of their camera up against it so that they're flooded with natural light. Never, ever do it the other way around, where your back is to the window. The viewer will only see your silhouette.

Relying exclusively on natural light is risky because of, well, clouds. They move around and block your light, sometimes while you're shooting. Plus, if the only time you have to tape is after dark, the window trick isn't going to work.

When you're ready to graduate from using windows, most people start with a ring light. They're inexpensive and have space for a camera or phone to be mounted inside of them. Consider getting one that's dimmable. It's always better to have more customization than less. Ring lights are popular but tend to reflect bright circles in actors' eyes, which can be a little distracting to some viewers. Also, they aren't for lighting up large areas. You'll need something more if you want to move around and interact with your space.

LED panels are a great choice. Some are multicolor, run on batteries, and come with remote controls so you can make adjustments without having to leave your spot in front of the camera. Panels are sometimes sold in kits, and if you're going that route, think about getting a set of three. You'll be able to execute a three-point light setup, which can level up the look of your auditions. If that sounds like too many, two panels will be just fine.

For higher budgets, take a look at LED spotlights that can be paired with soft boxes and other light diffusers. These pack a punch and are good for lighting up larger areas, but are expensive compared to other options. They're often sold without stands, so plan on adding them to your order.

Let's talk about your camera choice. The best camera for self-taping is the one you have! There's no need to buy anything fancy. The camera on your phone is probably great, and it can do double duty as an editor. Another option is to use a DSLR or mirrorless camera. These offer a lot more flexibility, but are pricey and make sense only if you already have one.

Whatever camera you choose, always make sure it's mounted on a tripod. The shot must be stable, never handheld. And there is no such thing as a selfie audition, so if you're using your phone, always mount it horizontally. With the exception of slates, don't shoot auditions vertically unless you're specifically asked to do so.

The Sound

It doesn't do any good to have a great-looking audition if no one can hear you. To make auditions sound their best, first consider your space. Ideally, you want to shoot somewhere that won't produce a lot of echoes. Avoid setting up in bathrooms, kitchens, and other places with hard surfaces like tiled floors and walls. These rooms allow sound to bounce around (also called "slapback"), which can be downright strange on camera.

Your recording device has a built-in microphone. It's better than nothing, but it is not your best choice. It's sound quality is lackluster, but the bigger issue is that onboard mics will always be where the camera is, not where you are. This is problematic for auditions with readers. Typically, a reader will be closer to the camera's mic since they'll be standing just to the side or behind it. With the auditioning actor farther away from the mic, the reader's voice is the most prominent one in the audition. That's not what you want. It's your audition, not theirs, so you want to have the louder voice.

Consider upgrading your setup with an external mic. There are a few ways to do this. The least expensive and probably most effective option is to go with a lavaliere mic, which is a mic that clips to your clothes. They're sometimes called "lapel mics," or "lav mics." These can usually be seen in the shot, but pick up your voice really well. They can be wired or wireless. Wired mics can be inexpensive, but you do have to be picky about which one you buy. The cable needs to be long enough to reach from your phone to your shirt. There's no need to spend extra money for wireless lav mics unless you plan to use them for things other than your auditions.

Another option is an external on-camera mic. These are sometimes made for specific products, like iPhones or iPads, but there's a greater variety of them made to work with DSLRs and mirrorless cameras. They tend to be directional, which means they pick up sound from one direction instead of from anywhere in the room. This is good because they automatically amplify your voice better than that of your reader. They also free you from the wire that comes with a lapel mic, and are not visible in the scene since they're attached to the camera. Whichever you choose, make sure to look at the mic's connector. You may have to buy an adapter to make it work with your particular device.

The File

Wouldn't it be great if doing an audition was as simple as pressing record, acting, pressing stop, and emailing a file? Unfortunately, it's not that simple. There is no standard yet for saving, labeling, and transmitting your audition. Everyone wants something different! It's important to read the instructions that come with each audition and follow them to the letter.

Some auditions ask for one file, meaning that if you have a slate, it'll have to be included with your scene(s). If you're using a phone or tablet, it will come with an app like iMovie that allows you to edit the footage. There are also external apps that may have more features. If you shoot with a regular camera, you'll need to get the footage into your computer for the edit. You can use anything from Filmora to Adobe Premiere Pro as an editor.

Whatever software you choose, there are a couple of things to keep in mind. Generally, viewers want these files to be free from distractions, so avoid putting graphics, text, and lower thirds over the image. You can experiment with different kinds of transitions from scene to scene, but it's best to keep them as simple as possible. You should also avoid applying any filters to the image. It's fine to do something simple like lighten or darken it, but stay away from doing anything that significantly alters the picture.

When you have your audition edited, check the email or casting notice that came with the audition for details about where the file(s) should be sent, how many to send, how it (they) should be labeled, and size limits. Some offices want one file with the slate and all the scenes put together. Others want the slate and scenes saved and sent as individual files. Sometimes we're told exactly what to name the file, and other times we're not. Some folks need you to limit the file size to less than 100MB, and others don't want files at all—they would rather you post the audition to Vimeo or YouTube.

File size is a consideration. Make sure the default settings on your recording device aren't set to shoot 4K or at very high frame rates. 1080p, 30fps is just fine. Anything higher generates files that will be too large for many casting systems to accept, and you'll have to downgrade them before submitting.

There are several movie file types currently accepted by the industry: .avi, .mov, and .mp4 are the most common. I like .mp4. Your editing software will probably allow you to convert your file type from one to another, but if it doesn't, a free app like HandBrake can help. You'll notice that the file size will adjust with each type. An .avi will be larger than an .mp4.

Some agents prefer that you send them your file, which they'll then upload after having a look. You'll need a way to transmit something that's likely too big to email. I use a site called WeTransfer.com. It lets you send up to 2GB for free, and it does so flawlessly. You can also save your files to a cloud storage system like Google Drive, Dropbox, or any other service and send viewers a download link.

Readers

Most scenes involve at least one other character besides yours, so you'll need someone else to help you with the audition. It's great if you can get an actor friend to be your reader, but anyone will do in a pinch.

What are your options if you can't get someone to be your reader in person? You bring them in virtually, of course! This usually requires having two devices running (one to shoot and one showing the virtual reader), but you can do your audition this way if it's the only way it'll get done.

When you bring in a virtual reader, make sure you're positioning them as you would a reader who is in the room with you. Put them off to one side of the lens, and behind it a little. You want to be able to see them, but you don't want the second device right next to your camera unless you're using an external mic. Electronic voices seem to cut through even more so than human voices in the room, so make sure yours is the loudest the audience will hear.

Tips and Tricks

The great thing about auditioning at home is that we have control over our environment. That means we can set it up how we like it to ensure we're as comfortable as possible.

My routine involves adjusting the temperature to my liking, having water nearby, and posting scripts where I can see them. I usually type out the scripts into a new document using a large font size, allowing me to easily see the words from farther away. I'll print them out and tape them to light stands, tripods, wherever my eye line will be during the scene. I also keep a chair nearby in case there's some waiting time involved during a virtual callback.

I know the routines of my neighborhood pretty well and try to shoot around times like trash pickup, landscape services, and when kids are getting home from school. My setup is pretty solid but outside noise can still get in from time to time. And if an ambulance drives by during a take, I just begin again.

Want More?

Visit ActingCareerMentor.com for my free self-tape resource guide. It has some specific equipment suggestions for all budget levels. Bottom line: if you can't produce a decent self-taped audition, pay an acting school, taping facility, or coach to make sure your tape looks and sounds as good as possible. But honestly, there's no reason why actors can't master the art of submitting a great self-tape.

Actor Reels and Clips

The industry uses headshots, resumes, and auditions to get to know actors, but there's another tool that has become even more influential. It's the actor's reel.

A reel is a collection of video clips, or scenes, that show the actor as they appear in finished projects. This way, casting can actually see an actor's work instead of trying to imagine what they might do from a headshot. Reels and clips are valuable. They can mean the difference between an actor getting an audition or being passed up for one.

Ideally, reels should be made up of scenes from actual films and TV shows, commercials, or other types of work in which the actor was cast. For those new to the business, this is something to aim for. Until an actor has gotten some of this work, they can use footage from acting classes, auditions, student films, or other less formal productions.

It's been standard practice for actors to assemble a reel from a few different clips. In total, there might be three or four scenes totaling two or three minutes in length. However, lately there's been a movement to use individual clips instead of entire reels.

Online casting sites allow actors to post clips to their profiles. Casting finds it more efficient to see shorter clips with descriptive titles that describe the kind of role the actor plays in the scene. For example, "Actor Name—Bartender" or "Actor Name—Rookie Cop." This way, casting can find exactly what they need without scrolling through a longer reel for the section they need to see. Actors can save their full-length reels for their own personal websites.

Once you have quite a bit of work under your belt, you'll have a separate reel for each work category. A look at chrisagos.com will show you what I mean. I have separate reels for TV/film, commercials, and industrials. It's not a good idea to combine different work categories in one reel. Keeping them separate helps viewers easily find what they're looking for.

Chapter Ten

Social Media

Our social media landscape is constantly evolving. Individual platforms rise and fall, but the larger world of social media has staying power. For actors, that means it's an opportunity that might be too good to pass up.

Actors use visibility to help propel our careers forward. We have to be seen, either by audiences or players in the industry that can put us in front of audiences. In the past, the only way to do this was by getting lots of auditions and booking a nice, juicy job. Today, social media solves this problem, allowing us to develop an audience on our own.

There are plenty of stories about casting decisions coming down to two actors, with the job ultimately going to the one with the larger social following. Producers figure that if an actor comes with a built-in audience, some of those eyeballs are going to watch whatever project the actor does. That may or may not be true, but it's the perception that matters.

Beyond follower counts and engagement numbers, producers look at the social profiles of actors to get a feel for who we are. It's an easy way for them to make sure we fit with their project. This is especially true if we're being considered commercially. Brands tend to hire people who will resonate with their customers, and our socials can become a tool in their casting process.

Because of this, the quality of an actor's profile is important. Focusing on the numbers at the expense of quality content can backfire. The thing to remember is that having a large social following is neither required to have an active career, nor is it a guarantee of future work. Casting decisions usually still come down to the actor who's most right for the job based on an audition, especially in smaller markets. But we need to do something with our socials.

If you're like me and you're not terribly invested in social media, you can start small. There are some best practices to consider.

Best Practices

I'm not a social media guru, so maybe consider other sources if you're looking for a deep dive. I'll cover some commonsense basics of social media use as it pertains to a new actor's career.

If you're starting fresh, do a sweep of whatever public profiles you have. Make sure they are indeed public. Profiles set to "private" won't be discoverable, going against the whole idea of having profiles in the first place. Make sure there's nothing posted you'd rather people not see. Those old party pics should probably go, unless you'd like them to be part of your online brand. Some actors start new profiles for their acting work.

When my wife was growing up in rural Illinois, her mother had a great saying: "Never do anything you don't want to read about in the newspaper." Replace the newspaper with the internet, and that's still good advice today. Our social profiles are like our headshots and resumes. They represent us when we can't be there in person, so they should match what we'd bring to an in-person meeting.

Next, turn off location sharing on all your profiles. Actors of all experience levels have privacy concerns. You can always add location information to a post, but you should turn off the setting that does it automatically.

Decide how you're going to use social media. There are actors who use it professionally, personally, or a mix of both. Those who stick with promoting their skills and work sometimes have different accounts for their personal use so they can post content that isn't meant for potential employers.

Different platforms are useful for different content. Instagram is great for photos and videos. So is TikTok, but those videos are going to be shorter. Twitter/X, is great for text and tends to be more popular with comedians and writers (who seem to be migrating to Threads). Facebook does a little of everything and seems to be the leader for engagement. There are other platforms out there, and by the time you read this, I'm sure there will be a new one of the moment. The point is that we need to be familiar with the strengths of the largest players.

Cross-posting to multiple platforms can sometimes backfire. If I see the same photo being posted on Instagram, Facebook, and all the others, by the third time I encounter it, I want to unfollow that actor because they're spamming my feeds with repetitive content. Be mindful that social media moves quickly and new content is most valued. A post will have legs for maybe a day or two, and then viewers move on.

YouTube can be considered social media, but it's used in a different way than other platforms. Content there is either entertainment or instructional. Actors often use it to post reels, clips, and other examples of their work. Same with Vimeo, though it tends to be for more professional users.

Figuring out what to post is one thing, but knowing when not to post is just as important. The general rule is that we can't post content that isn't ours. That means we shouldn't post our auditions because they are confidential and not for public consumption. The producers of that project do not want their script splashed all over social media. They want it to be released on their terms, not ours. So never, ever post anything about your auditions, and that includes the fact that you got to audition at all.

Once we're hired, we need to be careful about posting photos taken on the set, or behind the scenes. Every production has different rules about what can be posted and when, so make sure you ask for permission to post even the most mundane of content. The includes everything from costumes, to sets, to crew members doing their jobs. You can take photos, just don't post them unless you're cleared to do so.

Some sets have such strong security around photos and videos that actors have to turn in their phones before they work. Recording devices are kept in lockers until lunch or the end of the day or when the actor's released from set. Secrecy is a big thing now.

Once the project has been released, production will often let actors post clips of their appearances, but be sure to get their permission. Remember, even though it's your face, it's someone else's content, so make sure they're OK with you posting it.

Social media is great for making and maintaining connections, which can sometimes lead to real-world jobs. What social media shouldn't do is become your main thing. It can become a grind, so don't let it replace the work of being an actor. Being a social media star is very different from being an actor. The industry has discovered this multiple times. For a while, YouTubers and influencers were being cast in scripted projects over actual trained actors. The results weren't always positive, which is why producers have become more careful about casting them.

Don't feel like your social accounts are a make-or-break part of your career. I've seen actors post content daily, stuff that clearly takes a lot of time, planning, and effort. Whether that translates into paying acting work, I don't know. But it does send a message that the actor is more of a social media entity than anything, which might make some clients pause before hiring them. Perception means a lot. If our goal is to have an acting career, consider that our time might be better spent in class honing our craft.

Action Items

Things you can do right now:

- Begin researching headshot photographers.

- Choose one to meet with or talk to, even if you're not ready to schedule a photo shoot.

- Get the resume template at ActingCareerMentor.com.

- Begin thinking about your "special skills" list.

- Investigate online casting services. Open accounts. Have a look around inside.

- Work as a background artist on a production. Check local Facebook groups for opportunities.

- Look around your house and determine where you might tape an audition.

- Pick up one part of a self-tape kit: a light or a portable background, something to get started.

- Experiment with your new purchase and your phone's camera.

- Download trial versions of video editing software and play around with them.

- Look through your closet and choose some things that could be in your on-camera wardrobe.

- Register your name with all social platforms just to make sure you have it.

- Follow me @chrisagos everywhere. My handle on YouTube is @ChrisAgosActor

- Consider registering www.yourname.com if it's available. Other domains like .tv work, too.

- If you've already done some work, track down copies of the finished product.

Part 3

The Relationships

Chapter Eleven

Agents

I n our careers, we'll interact with two important groups of people: partners and clients. Our partners are the people who benefit directly from our success, like agents and managers. We can also put casting directors on this list, because they benefit from our good work at their auditions. We work together with our partners to create opportunities.

Our clients include everyone who has ever hired us. From directors to ad agencies, producers to print photographers. When we help them achieve their goals, they want to work with us again.

Each group has a different set of expectations. Our partners want open communication, accessibility, and an equal distribution of work. Partnerships fall apart unless each side holds up their end of the relationship.

Clients want good service. Acting is a creative endeavor, but it's also a service-oriented business. Anyone who has hired someone knows that *how* the job is done is just as important as the *final result*. If we make the job harder than it has to be, we'll have unhappy clients.

Working with Agents

Actors often think agents get them work. Nope. Agents get us auditions, but we still have to convince the client to hire us. The agent connects us to potential jobs, but they don't make the final casting decision.

An agent's job is to facilitate the work that comes across their desk. Clients who want to hire actors contact agents, describe what they're looking for, and the agent auditions the talent who might be right for the job. Or, casting directors call agents looking for talent, and the agent sends actors to their auditions. Once we've gotten the job, the agent negotiates our pay, coordinates the logistics of the booking, collects payment from the client, and then pays us. From the time we get the audition notice to the time we're paid, all the information about that booking will come through the agent.

Actors can work with agents in two ways. We can be exclusive, or multi-listed. The dominant format around the country is the exclusive rule, meaning that when an actor signs with a talent agency they are committed to that one agency for a particular kind of work. For example, if an actor is with Agency A for film, TV, and theater (also known as legit work in NYC), they will audition for that work category only with that agency. However, they would be able to have a different agent for other work categories like commercials or voice over.

It's possible for an actor to have multiple agents exclusively in different cities. For example, an actor with Agency A in Los Angeles might have a different agent in Atlanta submitting them for the same type of work. That kind of arrangement requires open communication between both agents to prevent overlap.

There are various types of talent agencies. Some are specialists, focusing on just one kind of work, or one category of performer. Maybe they only represent actors for film and TV work, or focus on representing minority actors. These types of agencies are often located in large markets. There are also full-service agencies that represent all types of talent for every work category. These are the norm in smaller markets.

In certain cities, like Chicago, an actor can be multi-listed. This means they can be signed with as many agencies as will take them for the same kind of work. Auditions may come from all of them, and none can claim the actor can't work with anyone else. This sounds like a great idea until you have too many agents that start to conflict with each other. If four agents call you for the same audition, you have to tell three of them you're already on it with another agency. That tends to frustrate agents.

Which way is best? Well, it depends on the market. In large cities where exclusivity is the rule, actors really don't have a choice. In theory, being exclusive with an agent is a good thing. It means more individual attention. The actor occupies a certain position in the agency's talent pool and should be submitted for anything in that actor's wheelhouse. Being multi-listed doesn't come with this assumption. Actors with multiple agents sometimes get lost in the shuffle unless they draw attention to themselves by booking a lot of work.

You'll encounter agencies that only work with actors on an exclusive basis, and those that don't offer exclusivity to anyone. There are also agencies that prefer to work on a hybrid basis, meaning they don't mind if an actor is with one or two other agencies.

There are times when an agent will want a trial period with an actor before committing to them for the long term. This is sometimes called a handshake deal, or "hip-pocketing." It means that the actor is not exclusive, but working with the agency anyway. I'm a fan of this practice since it gives both the agent and the actor a feel for what it's like to work with each other. These trial periods can last for a few months to a year.

When an actor signs exclusively with an agent, the agreement typically lasts eighteen months. Some agents will offer twelve-month deals, while others will ask for three years. I recommend a time frame somewhere in the middle. A year may not be enough time to allow things to develop, and I would hesitate to put my career in the hands of someone I've just met for three years.

Some agencies agree to work with actors without a written contract. Others take a more formal approach and present them with written agreements spelling out all the terms of the deal. If you're asked to sign anything, read it thoroughly before you do. You want to know if there is an auto-renew provision, what termination rights you have, and other details that will impact your experience with that agency. Don't sign anything without first reading it.

Talent reps can't legally charge a fee to represent an actor until that actor works a job that the agent helped them to secure. If you ever come across someone who wants you to pay them before you book any work, walk away from that person. Run, if you are able. You should never pay a membership fee, or any other fee, for representation. Agents are only owed a commission after you work.

That being said, some agencies maintain company websites where they list their talent and charge them to have their photos and videos uploaded to the site. We're usually asked to pay this fee before we do any work. This is legal and does not signal that we're being ripped off. The truth is that clients are perusing the agency's sites fairly often, so being included will never hurt an actor. If the cost is reasonable, it's probably worth paying.

A successful actor–agent relationship is a partnership. The good reps keep this in mind. Actors sometimes think that they work for their reps, but this isn't the case. Talent representatives technically work for actors, though it can seem like the opposite since the power balance is tilted in favor of the agency. There is a limited supply of talent agents and a seemingly unlimited supply of actors, so competition for roster spots can be tough.

Talent reps decide which actors they would like to work with by setting goals for their agency. Some agents like to keep their roster small. Others focus on a particular type of talent, or actors with a certain level of experience, name recognition, or both. Every agency maintains a talent pool, which is constantly shifting.

Getting an Agent

Agents typically find talent in one of two ways: through submissions or referrals. In general, agencies in large cities prefer referrals from other industry players like managers (which we'll talk about in a bit), and those in smaller markets accept actor submissions.

Without a referral, it's common for actors to send their materials to talent agencies, especially in smaller markets. When we're interested in a talent agency, we first visit the company's website and look for their submission policies. Some have a dedicated email address just for the purpose, and others prefer that materials are uploaded to a particular link. If there's no mention of submissions on the site, we'll call the agency and ask whoever picks up the phone. We then follow the instructions to the letter.

Submissions consist of a headshot and resume, a cover letter, and any other materials we may have like reels or VO demos. For more on voice over, see *The Voice Over Startup Guide*. It's best if the submission contains links to these things. Be careful when attaching large files to emails because many inboxes will reject them.

If you don't have an industry connection to refer you to an agent, let's look at the submission process that's worked for me and countless others, step by step.

1. Submit your headshot, resume, and other materials to the agent however they want to receive them. Your cover letter should be short and to the point. You don't have to sell yourself here; a simple introduction is fine. Something like this:

Dear Claire,

I'm an actor looking to expand my employment potential in our market, and Clarie's Talent could be a good fit. I'd love to meet with you (virtually or in person) and discuss how we might begin a mutually beneficial relationship.

My headshot and resume are attached, but if you'd like to see my past work, visit my website or IMDb page, where you can view reels and clips. If you think there's a place for me in your talent pool, I'd love to talk about joining the agency.

Thanks,

Chris Agos

(312) 555-1212

my@emailaddress.com

2. Wait. This is the hardest part because you're anxious for an answer if one doesn't immediately come. The agent could have looked at your stuff and decided you weren't right for their agency, or it could be lost in their inbox or in a submission folder on some cloud server. If you haven't heard anything from them after a month, send another note, one that's a little different. Try something like this:

Dear Claire,

About a month ago, I sent you a headshot and resume for consideration by Claire's Talent. I'm still interested in pursuing a mutually beneficial relationship with the agency, and would love to read for you. Have a look at my reels at chrisagos.com. If you're interested, feel free to get in touch. Have a great day!

Chris Agos

(312) 555-1212

my@emailaddress.com

3. Wait some more. Resubmit every month for six months, keeping your overall tone positive and upbeat, even if it's your sixth letter and you're ticked off that no one's gotten back to you. At the six-month

point, assume they can't use you right now. But you never know, you may get a call down the road.

The process is the same if you're submitting to an agent that only represents talent for VO. They probably won't want a headshot or resume, but do include a cover letter much like the examples above.

A lot of agents representing actors for on-camera work also do print, especially in smaller markets. If you're interested in doing that, explore it with them after the agent expresses an interest in you. If you've already done some print work and have a comp card (a collection of looks you can pull off successfully), send it along with your headshot. If you're looking to do trade shows, the process is much the same.

Some agents have very little time during an average workday to look at all the submissions they get, so they set them aside to consider every so often. Some do this twice a year, some maybe every quarter. That means you should expect some time to pass before you get a reply. If you follow this system, they'll have six chances over the course of half a year to see your name. Someone will eventually look at your stuff.

Did you notice that the process does not include walking into agents' offices? Agents don't like drop-ins, and these days many of them don't even have office spaces to walk into. If they do, walking in will not help your case. Allow time for your submission to go through their internal process. If you feel like you just have to do more than send something once a month, you can inform them of other career-related things you might be up to, especially if you're doing theater, improv, or stand-up. You want to be persistent, but not annoying. It's a fine line.

They Reached Out! Now What?

Agencies onboard new talent in a few different ways. Some start with a meeting, which could happen in person or virtually. It's a chance for agents and actors to get to know each other. In this situation, try to relax and be yourself. Ask about things like exclusivity and the various corners of the business the agents work in. You just want to see if you can get along with the people on the other side of the desk.

Sometimes you'll be asked to audition at these meetings. This happens more in smaller markets, but there may be a cold reading or some other audition the agency uses to screen talent. If you're given advance notice of this, plan for it like you would a regular audition. If the agency is large enough, the other agents may view the tape at a later date. Sometimes they don't take on a new actor unless every agent in the office approves the addition.

Some agencies will skip the meeting and ask you to register with them. This basically involves you filling out an online form so they can start submitting you for work. In these cases, there's less investment on the agency's side. New actors are put on a list, and they're submitted as often as possible, but it can be tough to have an actual relationship with anyone in the office.

We want to give our new agents every opportunity to think of us when they have something for which we're right. We can do that by checking in with them. This is a term from the old days when actors would physically drop by their agents' offices. Sometimes they'd bring coffee, other times they'd just come in to chat, but the subtext was always the same. What they were really doing was putting in some face time with their agents. If you're top of mind, you're more likely to be submitted for projects.

Today, keeping in touch doesn't involve dropping by anyone's office. We can try to connect with them via email or social media. Just ask which they prefer, and don't overdo it.

What if They Don't Call?

There's one universal truth about all agencies: they're in business to make money. In order to make as much as possible, they need to have a list of actors they think will give them the best shot at booking work. Keep in mind that when an actor goes on an audition, they're auditioning against other actors who are represented by other talent agents. So not only is that actor competing for the job, but the agent is, too.

Sometimes, the agent is happy with the group they have and doesn't feel the need to add anyone else. But people move, switch agents, or otherwise become unavailable. When there's a hole in the talent pool, agents are more open to meeting new actors, but only ones that can plug the hole.

Let's say an agency works with about two hundred actors. The group is evenly split between men and women, and there's a good age range from young to old. Lately there's been a lot of actresses in their thirties having babies, which takes them out of the loop for a while. Suddenly, instead of having plenty of women in that age range, the agency has a shortage. They need to find women they don't know to take the place of the new moms. The agents turn to the submissions they regularly get, but look only for women in their thirties. They don't need anyone else at the moment. If you don't fit that profile, you won't be contacted.

This is good to know because so many actors take it personally when an agent doesn't respond to their request for representation. Actors feel like there's something wrong with them, or that they're somehow not good enough. If an agent passes you over, that doesn't say anything about your headshots, your ability, look, or talent. It might just mean that they have enough people who compete with you.

If you know you're doing everything you should be doing, then don't take it too seriously when agents aren't snapping you up. Not all agents are looking to add new people, nor are they always looking for your type.

Maintaining the Relationship

While you're working with your new agent, the number one thing to remember is to be professional. You're in the business world, even though it's a creative business. Use common sense and put your best effort forward all the time, not just in the audition room. Part of being professional means being easy to reach. Sometimes auditions come with very little notice. Don't assume they can wait; assume they needed you yesterday.

Being professional also means showing up where you're supposed to be and on time. If you're driving to a physical audition, remember to allow enough time for traffic and parking. If it's a virtual audition, you have even less of an excuse to be late.

Despite our best efforts, sometimes things happen. If you're going to be late to an audition, call your agent first regardless of which type it is. If you're really late, it's possible you might not be able to audition at all. Let your agent find out for you.

If you're going to be late for a job, again, call the agent who booked you. When you're on the set be cordial and focused, getting the job done in a way that will make the client call your agent and compliment your work. That's how you'll get more auditions and jobs.

After a booking, some agents like you to check in with them. They want to know how it went, but they're also interested in knowing how many hours you worked in case you went into overtime. Overtime usually means more pay, so they use your word of what happened on the set as the basis for billing the extra time. If you're a union actor, keep track of how long your lunch break was, and how many of your wardrobe choices the client used if they asked you to bring any, since there are fees associated with that. These are all things that may determine the final amount you earn for the job. Some agents don't require you to tell them this, so if you're not sure, just ask what they prefer.

Staying Available

More than anything, being a professional actor means that you are available to work and audition. By declaring to the world that you deserve to be paid for your services, you simply must be available to do your job. Nothing is more frustrating to an agent, and nothing will end the relationship faster, than if you're habitually not able to perform the duties of a working actor. Remember, auditions and jobs will happen from nine to five, Monday through Friday. If you have a full-time job, hopefully it's flexible enough that you can skip out when necessary. This is why you hear about actors supplementing their acting work with other jobs that don't have regular schedules, like restaurant or gig work.

When you know you're not going to be available to audition or work, let your agent know. This is called "booking out." You book out for vacations, survival jobs, even acting classes. If it's going to prevent you from acting during the workday, you can book out for it. Some agents want you to book out for everything, while others just want to know when you're going to be out of town. Check with them to find out their preferences.

Payday

Once you've done a job, it's OK to ask your agent how long it might take to be paid for it. If the agent has a history with the client, they might be able to give you an estimate. If you're a union actor, there are safeguards in place that assure you'll be paid within a month, although sometimes it can take a little longer. If you're nonunion, it could take quite a bit longer, up to 120 days. The money has to go through several entities before it winds up in your hands. The company you worked for has to be paid by their client, which might have to get a check from somewhere else. Once your agent gets a check, they'll pass one along to you.

We'll be learning a lot more about getting paid in a later chapter, and we'll get very specific about numbers.

Head Games

In times when business is booming and you feel like you're in a groove, you'll love your agent(s). You'll feel like you're a valuable gear in a well-oiled machine. When times are slow and you're wondering where all the auditions are, you'll feel like the machine has rusted to a halt and you won't know why. It's easy to blame them. You might think they're deliberately hiding work from you, or that they just don't like you anymore.

Actors are good at assuming things. I think that comes from having no insight into what goes on in your agent's office from day to day. Agents don't publicly share much about what their actors are up to because that information is between the agent and the talent. No one but the agents actually know if they're busy, or if clients need actors of your type, or if the casting directors have anything in the works. We just assume that projects are falling into their laps left and right.

This is totally understandable. Seeing the business as being filled with potential helps actors deal with its uncertainty. We have to believe there's enough work for everyone, because if there isn't, how will there ever be enough for us?

While it's true that jobs happen every single day, there are times when it's just really slow. That has nothing to do with you, nor does it have anything to do with your agent or your agent's view of you. It simply means they don't have anything for you at the moment.

Do agents drop talent? Yes. But when it happens, it's for a reason, and you'll be told why. But if you don't get that kind of email, just assume there's simply nothing available for you at the moment. Check in as often as they've welcomed you to, and stay positive that good things will happen.

The Party's Over

Is there ever a time to break up with an agent? Yes. If you're multi-listed, and you've got an agent or two that you never hear from, why waste time and energy on them? You don't want to hit the break-up button too quickly, but if you've been holding up your end of the deal by keeping in touch, following their policies, and staying available for anything that might come up, you should eventually get some positive reinforcement. If you don't, do you really want to be with that agent?

A long time ago, I was registered with an agency but just wasn't getting calls from them. One day I was doing some background work on a commercial. I was part of a crowd scene, and a nice lady was positioned next to me. We started chatting, and I learned that she worked part time at this agency. I mentioned that I was with them, and she looked at me funny.

She said, "Really?" With one word she basically confirmed that I wasn't in their loop at all.

I nodded and told her I hadn't been contacted for anything since registering. Aloud, she wondered why. I just kept shrugging because I didn't have a clue. By the time this exchange happened, she had worked with me the whole day and knew I was good on a set and a nice person. That was all she needed.

"Do you have any headshots on you?" she asked. I did, and gave her a couple. She eyeballed my resume, and explained why I may not have been called yet.

"You're pretty young, and a lot of what we get goes to older guys. Also, it can just be hard for new people to break through. The agents have their list of people they know they can count on, so they usually just call in the same actors, especially if there are only a few spots available. If an actor does a bad audition, the agent just looks like they don't know how to do their job." She looked at me for a second as I nodded along with her reasoning.

Finally she said, "I'll see what I can do." The next week, I had an audition at her office. And not long after that, I booked a client that brought a lot of work to the agency. From that point on, I was on their short list. I don't know who I bumped off it, but I'm glad there was room for me.

I've said that perseverance is the key to being successful in this business, but there's also a time for a reality check. If you've got an agent who simply won't allow you to play the game, you have the right to walk off the field. How long you wait to do that is up to you, but I'd say eighteen months is a good amount of time. If it's been a one-sided relationship that whole time, the situation seems unlikely to change. You'll have enough uncertainty in this business, and you don't need it from someone who's supposed to be supportive.

There are other reasons to break up with an agent. One actor told me about an agent who used his computer skills more than his acting skills. The agency would call him when their internet was down, or when they were having issues with their website, but they wouldn't call him to audition for anything. After a while they started giving his name out to actors who needed their reels edited. He dumped them, and rightly so.

If you have problems getting paid from your agent, you should make a change. Good agents know that they didn't earn that money, you did, and it belongs to you, not them. It's reasonable that they won't pay you until they get paid, but if you consistently have to wait five, six, seven months (or more!) to get a check for your work, why would you continue to give them interest-free loans? You're an actor, not a bank.

Most agents are terrific and work hard for the actors they represent. Keeping tabs on the relationship is just another part of our job because things don't always go the way we think they should.

Chapter Twelve

Managers

T alent managers can be an important part of an actor's team. Managers are generally more focused on the long-term aspects of an actor's career, while agents are more about the short term.

Managers typically act as a guide through the industry. They help actors with everything from headshots and marketing to finding agents. They're also supposed to introduce actors to key decision-makers who can advance their career. In this way, the manager engineers the actor's progress. Once an actor is very busy, the manager will help in the selection of projects and look for ways to augment the actor's success. When the actor wins, the manager does, too.

Because of the individual attention required, managers typically take on fewer clients than agents. Some keep their rosters to just a few actors, where talent agencies will work with hundreds.

The question most new actors ask about managers is this: "Do I need one?" The answer, as you might expect by now, is complicated.

Manager Expectations

Managers mostly operate in Los Angeles and New York, and that's because those markets are large enough to make them necessary. Part of a manager's job is to cut through the noise and get you seen by the right people. They can be very helpful when there are thousands of people to wade through. In contrast, it's possible for actors to navigate smaller markets on their own. Also, much of the lower-visibility work that's available in smaller markets is not very interesting to managers.

Everyone does things a little differently, but in the early stages of an actor's career, managers tend to operate like super-involved talent agents. They'll go over headshots and online profiles, help with reels and websites, and submit the actor for roles through online casting systems. They may also recommend working with a specific talent agency. It's helpful if an actor's agent and manager work well together. If the opposite is true, the actor can get stuck in the middle, resulting in few benefits from either relationship.

Once everything is up and running, a manager may set up meetings between the actor and key individuals the manager thinks the actor should meet. Sometimes these are general meet-and-greets, and other times they are for specific projects. In this way, the manager tries to expand the actor's network, and thus their employment potential.

All of this usually doesn't happen quickly. With any talent rep, often there's a burst of activity in the beginning, and then things slow down to a more organically slower pace. It's good to keep your expectations in check.

Getting a Manager

You'll often hear that managers only work with actors by referral, and they do not accept submissions. This is generally true, although as with any rule, exceptions abound. There are plenty of stories of successful actor–manager relationships starting with actors reaching out to the manager. The truth is that everyone is looking to make a buck, and if a manager thinks they can make a few (or more) with an actor, it doesn't matter how the connection was made.

You'll also hear that actors shouldn't engage the services of a manager until there's something to manage. This is also generally true, but I would add that sometimes managers are more effective at advancing a new actor's career than a talent agent, specifically because it's a closer relationship.

Does that mean you should get a manager? Hard to say, but I don't believe a manager is necessary unless you're working in a very large market and you have some history and experience under your belt in some part of the entertainment industry. If you decide to pursue a relationship, the process is the same as the one you'd use to secure an agent. Reach out to them with your materials in the same way on the same time intervals, and see if you get a reply.

Expect to pay managers a commission of 10 to 15 percent of your gross earnings. This will be on top of the commission you're already paying your agent, meaning a large part of your earnings will go to commissions before it comes to you. For this reason, both relationships better be clicking along and producing results. It's expensive to double up on talent reps.

Moving On

There are as many stories of ineffective managers as there are of those who make a huge difference in an actor's career. I would use the same guidelines that I recommended for agents. If eighteen months go by and the relationship hasn't produced a lot of opportunities, it's time to move on.

A lot of managers work on a handshake deal and nothing more. If there's nothing signed between the two parties, you should be able to walk away without much trouble, though it can be slightly more complicated depending on the situation. Talent agents have plenty of experience unwinding professional relationships. If you trust yours and need answers, you can always ask them for advice.

Chapter Thirteen

Casting Professionals

W hen actors talk about their team, they rarely include the casting folks who bring them in to audition. But if you ask the casting professionals, they'll likely say that they and actors should all be working together toward the same goals. Everyone in this industry is dependent on one another.

It's worth noting the difference between an agent and a casting director. Agents represent actors and casting directors don't. A casting director is hired by a producer to narrow down the search for actors from the entire talent pool in their market (and sometimes nationally or even internationally). In pursuit of assembling the best cast for the project, they audition actors represented by many different agents. As such, there's no obligation to actors from the casting director's standpoint. Agents, on the other hand, do have a responsibility to work in the best interest of the actors they represent. Casting directors service clients while agents service actors. There is no such thing as a casting agent, so don't ever use that term.

The truth is that a casting department auditions for their job just like we do. When a casting team is hired for a project, they want to do the best job possible. Their choices are constantly being evaluated, and enough missteps can mean they lose their job. Sound familiar? Actors are constantly auditioning, even after we book the work! Actors are let go of productions all the time for various reasons. There are famous examples, like the actor who was initially cast as Marty McFly in *Back to the Future.* There are also examples that don't get much attention, such as the actor who was leading a TV pilot I once worked on. He was fired after the first table read, before a single frame of footage was shot.

This puts actors and casting on the same page. An actor who helps casting look good by doing a great audition is one who is invited back again and again.

Casting Guidelines

As new actors, it's helpful to know the informal, unwritten rules that can help put us on a good path with the casting department.

There is normally a layer in between casting and actors, and that's the talent rep. Let your agent or manager contact casting for any reason. If we need something from them, like if we have questions about an audition, we don't reach out to casting directly. We ask our reps do that for us. Of course, there are exceptions to everything. If an actor doesn't have a talent representative but wants to submit themselves for a project, the casting sites have a way for that to happen. Obviously if we don't have reps, we can converse with casting on our own.

When we book a role, all the information about the job will pass from casting, through our talent reps, to us. Most casting folks don't mind getting a note or some other thank-you from actors. Maybe stay away from gifts, but a nice email or card is just fine.

Actors sometimes market to casting professionals. This is typically something simple like sending a postcard or email if we're doing a play or appearing on TV. For some of us, marketing is key to getting back in front of a casting director who's previously cast us, or introducing ourselves to someone we've never met. Other actors let their agents and managers do their marketing.

Occasionally, casting offices will have "pre-reads." These are either general auditions where there are no specific roles being cast, or early first-round auditions for a particular project. In either case, they're a chance for the casting office to see actors they may not have seen before.

Some casting professionals offer classes or workshops in their spare time. These can be fine to attend, but know that the information presented will be specific to that casting person only. Everyone operates a little differently, so take what you hear with a grain of salt. Know that a different casting office might have other opinions and preferences. Also, realize that attending these events in no way guarantees you a future audition with the office or people doing the presentation.

Following a casting person on social media does not automatically increase your chances of being called in by the person behind that profile. Casting has an entire database of actors from which to pull talent, so they don't need to use social platforms unless they can't find an actor any other way. Social profiles are often used to vet an actor when they're being considered for a role, which means actors shouldn't post anything they wouldn't want potential employers to see.

Speaking of social media, I am very skeptical of casting professionals who spend a lot of time pushing videos out through their social channels. This content often has a "my way or the highway" feel to it. Be cautious of anyone who says their opinion is the only correct one out there. The entertainment industry is wide open to many points of view.

In the end, the best way to have a great relationship with casting is to knock your auditions out of the park. This starts with the understanding that casting and actors are working together for the good of the story that's on the page.

Chapter Fourteen

Clients

O ur clients include anyone who hires us. They're producers, directors, writers, production company executives, ad agency creatives, photographers, and anyone else who helps us earn a paycheck doing what we love.

As creative as it is, acting is still a service business. When someone hires us, despite all the talk about wanting the best actor for the role, there are other factors involved in our casting. One of them is the level of service we'll provide to the client.

When you hire someone to do something for you, what are you looking for? Let's say you hire a guy named Tim to mow your lawn. First off, you expect Tim knows how to do the job. If you want something specific done, you'll have tell him because Tim, like all people, can't read minds. But you don't expect him to need training in the art of lawn mowing.

You want the whole transaction to be smooth. If Tim shows up on time, gets right to work, and gives the job his full attention, that's good. Even better if he seems to want to be there. When he comes with ideas and suggests ways to make your lawn look nicer, you get the sense that he enjoys his work. Tim made the whole experience easy for you, which makes you want to hire him again.

In contrast, if Tim arrives late, tries to convince you that you don't want what you're asking for, does a sloppy job, and can't leave fast enough, you probably won't hire him again.

As actors, we want to give our clients a good experience. This idea of making the day easy for clients is more important than you might think. I sometimes get to know the people I work with well enough that I can ask them about what they look for when they hire talent. One thing that comes up repeatedly is this idea that in an audition, decision-makers want to feel like you're going to make their shoot easier, or at least that you're not going make it harder for them. One director said to me, "I just don't want to have to teach them anything." Clients are watching auditions through this lens or listening to VO auditions with this in mind.

Repeat Business

I believe actors should come to each job with a sense of, "How can I help?" This is true whether it's a local commercial, a corporate VO project, or a big studio movie. We're artists, but we're also problem solvers. Keeping this in mind can grow careers.

A few years ago, I wrote a blog post called "The Ten Commandments of Getting Hired Again and Again." You can read the whole thing on ActingCareerMentor.com, but I'm going to go through a couple of my favorite commandments here because they're so relevant.

- Thou shalt arrive prepared. There should be no reason to say this, but I've seen actors show up to set late, not knowing their lines, and asking questions that can be answered with a simple online search. These kinds of unnecessary things are time wasters for the crew. Don't be that person. Be prepared with everything you need at all times.

- Thou shalt be attentive and observant. On every job, just pay attention to what's going on. Don't make people ask you for things twice. Anticipate the needs of others. If you're standing in a spot where a grip is heading with a light, move out of the way. If you've only done one successful pass of the script in a VO job, offer to do another for safety. Don't just wait to be told to do everything. You're part of a machine, and you don't want to slow the machine down in any way.

And this one might be my favorite because this is how you really get an education in this business:

- Thou shalt listen. To everyone. The director, the ADs (assistant directors), the DP (director of photography), the PAs (production assistants), the grips, the sound department, the props people, the script supervisor, the costume department, the makeup and hair crew, and most importantly, to the other actors in your scene. All these people know more about where you should be, and when, than you do. So follow their directions and don't assume anything. If you listen, you will learn things you'll never be taught in a class. It will be the greatest education you can get, and you're being paid to get it. It's priceless.

Find the other commandments at ActingCareerMentor.com.

Building Community

Once clients find an actor they like, they generally keep them in mind for future work. We can help them think of us by doing a few simple things.

Keep in touch with them, but do it in an unobtrusive way. Some actors lean heavily into social media, using it to reach out to former clients. Others take a more formal marketing approach, where they send emails and mailers to keep their name in front of people. Still others will work their client list for referrals to other industry pros. It doesn't matter which method you use as long as you're comfortable doing it and can keep it up over the long term.

I've also known actors to launch newsletters, updating clients monthly on what they're up to. They mention everything from work they're cast in, to classes they're taking. This kind of approach only works if there's something for the actor to talk about in every newsletter, so consistency is key. We want to remind them of who we are and what we bring to the party.

The other thing we can do, and this is for actors who have been around a little while, is to find ways to link our past clients together. Maybe an ad agency copywriter is looking for feedback on their first feature script, or a commercial director needs help shooting a sizzle reel for a TV show idea. When we can help those who have helped us, we make our time in the industry more valuable for everyone. Sometimes it's just a matter of staying active in the business in some way, even if it means not appearing in the project, but helping it get off the ground.

I've been known to suggest my actor friends as possible talent to hire. I've also been the beneficiary of this, since I'm occasionally referred by others for work. No one does anything in this business alone. Everyone develops a team of people with whom they enjoy working. Acting is an extremely collaborative business. In fact, when things are slow for me, what I miss the most are the people. I miss being part of a team as we all work toward a common goal.

If you put in the work, over time your community will grow and your career will grow with it.

Action Items

Things you can do right now:

- Pull up a map for your local area. Do a search for "talent agents" and see who you find.

- Read up on all of them. Skip sites without much information.

- Do the same for talent managers.

- Do the same for casting offices.

- Once you have some names, head to IMDb and look them up there. See who they represent.

- Draft a submission cover letter to an agent.

- Follow a few casting directors on social platforms to get a feel for who they are.

- Think about how you'll keep in touch with future clients. What feels right to you? Social media? Newsletters?

- Consider ways to start growing a community of friends in the business.

Part 4

The Money

Chapter Fifteen

Performance Unions

W e can't have a discussion about money without first learning about unions. Since they are so influential in the industry, sooner or later every actor will have to think about whether to join one. There's a lot to consider, but I'm going to keep things as simple as possible.

In the US, there are two performance unions that protect and advocate for professional performers. SAG-AFTRA (Screen Actors Guild–American Federation of Radio and Television Artists) covers those of us who work in recorded media. Actors Equity Association (AEA) covers performers on stage in front of live audiences. Though some actors are members of both unions, SAG-AFTRA is more relevant to our discussion.

In Canada, ACTRA (Alliance of Canadian Cinema, Television, and Radio Artists) is the national union covering artists in recorded media in that country. Actors who are not citizens of Canada, but who are members of SAG-AFTRA, can work there without joining ACTRA since the two unions have a reciprocity agreement. That's helpful since many US-based movies and TV shows are made in Canada, in whole or in part.

The union's primary objective is to protect actors and their ability to earn a living wage. The union works out collective bargaining agreements with companies. These negotiations result in contracts, which spell out rules that both companies and actors agree to follow on a job, and after. The rules are designed with actors' interests in mind and address everything from pay rates, to working conditions, to health care. The union doesn't negotiate for actors individually (that job belongs to agents), but for the entire membership.

When we say that a union "covers" performers working a certain type of job, we mean that it has jurisdiction over that kind of work. It's like a territory. If you're in Chicago, you're in the State of Illinois, a territory. If you do a job where a camera or microphone is used to record your performance so it can be played back later, you're working in SAG-AFTRA's territory.

The union has jurisdiction over almost any type of recorded media and use you can think of, from TV, to movies, to audiobooks and video games. That's not to say that every project made in the US is a union project—far from it—but there are contracts for about a dozen different work types. The union does not cover trade shows or print work, although if there is a video component to those gigs, that could be covered.

Some actors think that once they join the union, they'll have all the work they can handle because the union will see to it that they're kept busy. This isn't true. Being a member of SAG-AFTRA does not guarantee that we'll get work, because the union isn't involved in the casting process. We still have to audition to get our bookings whether we're in a union or not.

Although the union has jurisdiction over most work categories, it takes two to tango. There are a number of trade organizations representing producers on the other side of those contracts. Member companies like ad agencies, movie studios, and production companies will make most or all of their content using the union contracts their trade associations negotiated. However, there are many companies that are not part of the union ecosystem, and as such, they're under no obligation to use union talent.

This has given rise to a nonunion production industry that flourishes nationwide for both on-camera and VO work. The nonunion world is robust and not going anywhere, and it's the place where most emerging actors begin their professional careers.

Becoming a union member is a rite of passage and a source of pride for many actors. To some, being in the union means that they've arrived. It's an acknowledgment that they're really a professional performer. Before you consider whether or not union membership is for you, it'll help to know what it's like to be a union actor, and how it differs from being nonunion.

Working as a Union Actor

Before anyone can work as a union actor, they first need to join. Since any union job is usually open only to existing members, actors have forever been frustrated by this catch- 22, wondering, "If I have to be in the union to work the job, but I need the job to become union, how will I ever be able to join?" This is a fair question.

While producers of union productions sometimes just want to audition union performers, they're often open to seeing nonunion actors, too. Casting directors, agents, and producers want to match the role with the best actor for it, and if a nonunion actor is the choice, so be it. I broke into SAG-AFTRA like a lot of other actors, by doing a commercial. I voiced a TV spot. Back then I was doing all nonunion work, but I was with an agent who worked on both union and nonunion projects. She put me on the audition and I shocked her by booking it. If you're looking to join the union, you'll have the chance every time you audition for a union project.

Members of AEA or other performance unions around the world can join without ever setting foot into a SAG-AFTRA production. Background players on union projects also have a route into the union through that work. Check the union's website for the most current policies about joining in these ways.

Taft-Hartley

Actors don't have to join SAG-AFTRA immediately upon getting their first union booking. In the United States there's a federal law called the Taft-Hartley Act that allows a month between when we work our first union job and when we have to join. Consider it a time to test drive what it's like to be a union actor.

Let's say we work our first SAG-AFTRA project on June 1. We're now in a new phase of our career. We're no longer strictly a nonunion actor; we're what's called "Taft-Hartley'd." Starting June 2, we can work as many union jobs as we can get for thirty days without joining. However, after June 30, our status shifts to "must join."

Most actors work their first union job and then don't book another one during their month of freebies. In fact, some actors wait years to join. This might be because they don't really want to be in the union. Or it could be that the stars haven't yet aligned for them, and they're still waiting to be offered their next union booking. It doesn't matter how much time lapses between our first job and the one that makes us a must join; our Taft-Hartley status never expires until we have a union card in our wallet.

Joining is not cheap. There's an initiation fee running into the thousands of dollars, and then there are membership dues paid every six months. The initiation fee is fixed, though it's a little lower in some states than others. Dues are calculated based on our incomes. The more we earn, the higher our dues, up to a cap. You can check the union's website for the latest information, or call your local SAG-AFTRA office. There are several around the country.

What to Expect

Being a member of SAG-AFTRA has a lot of advantages, most of which center on money. The union sets a minimum rate for each type of work. Producers must pay actors that minimum, which we call "scale," and no lower. This acts as a safety net for incomes since rates can't be negotiated lower under any circumstances.

In addition to strong rates and overtime, union actors have the opportunity to earn money while we're not physically working. That's due to the union's residual system. When you book a job on a commercial, film, or TV project, you're paid for your time on the set, otherwise known as a session fee. Union jobs are billed by the day, the week, the spot, or the hour depending on the project. Actors are also paid a usage fee. In other words, producers are buying a license to use your face or voice for a set period of time. That fee, which is separate from the session fee, is a residual payment. We just call them "residuals," and they are paid as long as the project is generating revenue for the company that made or licensed it. For some projects, that may be a few months. For others, it's decades.

The union contracts have several other benefits built into them. For example, often your agent's commission is paid by the client, not by you. So if you're owed $1,000, you'll get the entire amount, instead of $900. Sometimes this has to be negotiated ahead of time by your agent. The contracts also say that actors must be paid within thirty days of finishing the job. If you're not, you're owed a late fee. I've been paid in as little as a week.

Other perks for actors include a fee for wardrobe use. If you bring clothing choices to a job and end up wearing one for the shoot, you get a little extra money for your trouble. The producer also incurs a fee if you're made to work longer than six hours without a lunch break. It's called a "meal penalty," and it's there to discourage producers from working too long without a break. Also, if for some reason you're booked on a job and it gets canceled within twenty-four hours of your call time, you'll still be paid in full.

Union actors enjoy other advantages including discounts on various services, loans, and products, access to the union's own credit union, informative educational events, meet-and-greets with agents and casting directors, and of course free screeners and downloads of movies nominated for best picture in the union's award show. Yes, as a member of the union, you get to vote and help decide who wins a SAG award. Pretty cool.

Perhaps the most valuable thing many actors earn through the union is access to health insurance and retirement plans. When you're paid for your services, producers also make a contribution to help fund these plans. The amount varies, but it's about 20 percent of your fee for doing the job. This applies to both on-camera and voice over work. So if you're paid $1,000, the producer contributes about $200 to the plans.

Actors qualify for these plans by meeting minimum earnings requirements in any given year. Once you qualify, you can decide whether to participate, and if you do, you'll pay a reasonable quarterly premium. You're automatically enrolled in the retirement plan once you qualify for it. You can find the current minimum qualification levels for both plans on the union's website.

So with all these benefits, what does the union expect in return? In addition to paying the initiation fee and dues, actors are expected to follow Global Rule One, which states that no member may accept nonunion work. Once you join the union, you agree to step into that world and leave the nonunion one behind you. This makes sense, since joining is a step that advances an actor's career. Plus, if a union member makes themselves available as nonunion talent, why would producers ever hire them as a union member?

CHRIS AGOS

Working as a Nonunion Actor

Not everyone embraces union membership, and that's OK. Working as a nonunion actor is a great way to learn the ins and outs of the business, especially in smaller markets where there's less union work. The nonunion world has its challenges, but more than anything else it's a great place to get an education. I worked for years as a nonunion actor, and learned a lot about the business from people who wanted me to do well.

The work available is similar to that in the union world. Actors are needed for spots, industrials, and voice over work. Nonunion agents get called for print and trade show work as well. There's also promotional work, which is a general term for a wide variety of jobs like handing out samples of perfume in department stores or working a company-sponsored event on a golf course. These are jobs where you're not necessarily acting, but you're still required to be professional. Scripted TV shows and most feature films are union, so if you'd like to work next to some famous names on those projects, you'll eventually have to become a member.

The nonunion world is a fee-for-service place. In other words, we do a job and are paid for our time there, and that's all. There is no long tail of residual payments. However, in recent years nonunion agents have taken a cue from the unions and try to negotiate usage fees for their talent. These fees are called "buyouts," and they cover a specific amount of time. So the actor gets their session fee and a buyout for maybe a year's worth of use. Agents are not always able to get these additional fees, but when they do, they can double or even triple an actor's pay.

There's no wardrobe fee in the nonunion world, nor is there a meal penalty. Overtime is usually paid, but sometimes it isn't, and you'll be told when you're walking into a job that could last for eighteen hours. Also, when you're a nonunion actor you don't have access to health or retirement benefits from your acting work. Most nonunion agents have a cancelation fee in place so you're compensated for holding time open for a job.

The union has rules around how a piece of content can be used. If it's going to have a life beyond its original purpose, there will be a fee due to the actor for that new use type. Imagine you appear in TV show. One of your scenes is used in the episode for which you're hired, but it also shows up in a later episode as a flashback. You'll be paid for the original appearance, and you'll also get a session fee and residuals for the flashback episode, even though you only shot the scene once.

Unfortunately, there's no such rule in the nonunion world. If you shoot a commercial and the advertiser decides later to lift some of the footage into a different commercial, there's no guarantee you'd be paid for that additional use. You might get something if you saw the new spot, or if someone made you aware of it. But you would have to inform your agent, and they would have to go back to the client and try to get payment. They may or may not be successful. Generally, there are fewer protections for actors in the nonunion world.

It may sound like I'm not a fan of this way of working, but that isn't the case! While I think joining SAG-AFTRA is a good decision for many actors, I also know it may not be practical for everyone. Union work isn't available everywhere; it's mostly concentrated in large markets like Los Angeles, New York, Chicago, and Atlanta.

Also, work can be tougher to get when we audition in a larger, more experienced, and highly trained talent pool. It's completely normal to launch a career in the nonunion world before moving into union membership at a later date.

As an emerging actor, it's important to know as much about the profession as possible, which is why it's worth spending time on SAG-AFTRA here. The union is also important since it impacts the rates paid to actors on every type of job, even those that are not covered under a union contract. Next, let's get specific about those rates.

Chapter Sixteen

An Actor's Income

I f you skipped the previous chapter, do yourself a favor and read through it. Understanding pay rates will be a lot easier if you have some details about SAG-AFTRA.

I hope you're not getting into this career for the money because if you are, I promise there are better industries to explore. Don't get me wrong, you can make a boatload as an actor, but the money should come as a complement to the main attraction, which is your love of acting and all it allows you to do.

Many, many factors determine an actor's income level: how well the nation's economy is doing, whether or not an actor is union or nonunion, what kind of work the actor books, which agent (or agents) the actor is with, how long the actor has been in the business, or how well-trained the actor is. You get the idea.

We all know there's uncertainty in our business. What's interesting is that this applies to famous actors as well as the rank-and-file. Interviews with accomplished talent sometimes reveal that we all have to deal with the income roller coaster.

Sharon Wottrich, former owner of a voice over talent agency, tells stories about VO artists whose annual incomes rocketed to $750,000 virtually overnight and then crashed down to $250,000. These are extreme examples, but they illustrate the unpredictability of acting for a living. And if you're thinking, "I'd be pretty happy if I made $250,000," I'm with you. But if you lived a $750,000 lifestyle, a mere quarter million would seem pretty low. It's all relative.

You've learned about some common ways actors make money from their acting. As we unveil exactly how much you can make in each of them, keep in mind your own situation. If you're new to the business, think about where you can focus your training to get your share of the pie. If you're coming back after a hiatus, what skill set might you add that would result in a financial gain? Cash flow helps us keep moving forward.

Commercials

Actors all across the country count on commercials for at least a portion of their income. Union actors depend on the residuals to smooth out a bumpy income stream. Nonunion actors cite them as a reason they can avoid supplementing their acting income. The earning potential is higher for union talent, but nonunion actors can still make a pretty good buck for a day's work.

We'll start with the union contract rates. I'll use the most current ones, but they're renegotiated every three years. Should you need them, the rate sheets are available on SAG-AFTRA's website. The union also has a great YouTube channel with lots of educational content, so check there for an explainer on how the contract works.

SAG-AFTRA members currently earn a scale session fee of $783.10 per shoot day, per spot. Shooting two separate commercials in one day will trigger two session payments.

Calculating residual payments can be tricky because of the number of variables involved. It'll help to understand a few key concepts. I'll give you a brief overview of the most important ones, and then we'll go through a real-world example of how an actor's residuals are determined.

For years, advertisers have been moving away from traditional TV networks like NBC, ABC, and CBS. These are considered the broadcast networks, meaning their signals travel over the air and not through a wire.

Even though their role in an actor's pay is severely diminished compared to years past, the broadcast networks are still an important part of the advertising landscape. They are significant enough to have their own pay structure for residuals, called Class A. An example of this type of use occurs when a commercial airs from a network's national feed and goes to every network affiliate at the same time. These happen during live sports, morning shows, nightly news broadcasts, and the like.

In the past, most ad dollars went to these networks, but now advertisers spend much more on digital media. As a result, the union has categorized the different types of available digital media, and come up with a set of rates for each of them.

Traditional digital platforms include social media and places we used to think of as websites. Think Facebook, Instagram, even YouTube, although the premium version of YouTube is considered a streamer. Streaming platforms are those that stream content similar to the traditional broadcast networks, but over an internet connection. These are services like Apple TV+, Hulu, and Tubi.

The union has grouped some other digital platforms into a third category called gaming, AR/virtual worlds and emerging platforms. These include platforms like the Sony PlayStation, Meta's Oculus, and new platforms and devices that haven't yet been invented.

The cable networks represent a different platform. They're delivered to homes either via satellite or with a literal cable that runs from the street to the house. These are networks like CNN, HGTV, and Discovery, and they come in a package of channels. You may notice that some cross over into the streaming category with examples like NatGeo, which is part of Disney+.

Advertisers buy the right to use a commercial in cycles, or blocks of time. The contract allows for an advertiser to buy cycles that last four weeks, thirteen weeks, or one year. This is true across most media types, and there are separate rates for each type. This means that if a client wants to buy time on network, cable, and traditional digital, they pay three different rates, but they all are likely to be on the same cycle. A cycle usually begins the first day a commercial is used.

When a company hires you to be in their commercial, there's a time limit placed on their use of your likeness and voice. It's called the "maximum period of use (MPU)," and it is twenty-one months. It begins either the first day the commercial is used, or thirteen weeks after the last day of the commercial's production.

During the MPU, you may get holding fees. These "hold" you for a product category and enforce a product conflict, meaning you can't appear in commercials for competing brands. Your session fee is considered your first holding fee, but additional holding fees are due every thirteen weeks during the MPU if your commercial is not airing anywhere. If it is being used, then your holding fee may not be due until one year after the last day of your shoot, or the one-year anniversary of the first day the commercial was used, whichever is earlier. Holding fees are typically applied as credits to residual payments. More on that later.

You'll get holding fees for commercials produced for all media types except for traditional digital platforms and gaming, AR/virtual worlds and emerging platforms. As such, there can be no exclusivity for commercials that only run on these platforms. If there's no conflict in place, you can work for the brand's competitors while your commercial is running.

An Example

Let's say you're hired to do one TV spot for a large national retailer. They're based in Minneapolis, so they fly you there for your shoot. You'll be paid a session fee for the travel day, and let's assume the shoot took one day of work and they flew you home that night. That means the total for your session is $783.10 times two, or $1,566.20

The retailer wants to get some Class A use, so they buy a package of placements from the networks. Class A is paid by the use. Your session fee includes the first use, but after that, you're paid on a sliding scale. Here it is:

Class A Rates

1st use: $783.10

2nd use: $183.19

3rd use: $145.33

4th–13th each use: $145.33

13-use guarantee: $2,242.42

14th–18th each use: $137.37

Each time the spot runs, you'll be paid a certain amount for that particular airing, and the rate decreases with each one. There's an option for the advertiser to buy a package of thirteen uses, representing one airing per week of a thirteen-week cycle, so let's assume they pick this option. That means $2,242.42 is coming your way. There is a cap on Class A payments of $20,000 in any thirteen-week cycle.

The latest contract contains a new flat-rate compensation system. We used to calculate our residuals by determining where the spot runs and how many eyeballs could potentially see it. But now, we're paid a flat rate for just about anything except Class A.

In a thirteen-week cycle, the retailer certainly wants to get the ad out there more than thirteen times. Doing that gets expensive with Class A, so they'll likely do it with cable, a more affordable option. Since they're a big company, they buy time at the national level. There are options to buy local cable, too, but that's for smaller advertisers.

They want the full boat, so they'll pay $4,100 for thirteen weeks of unlimited airing on national cable channels.

For digital platforms and streaming. remember that there are three different media types, but only two sets of flat fees for them. This is because use in the third category (gaming, etc.) is included when an advertiser pays for use on streaming platforms. The retailer wants to place their ad everywhere, so they pay $1,100 for traditional digital use, and $2,550 for streaming use.

Let's put it all together. Your session was $1,566.20. The total for the all the uses on a thirteen-week cycle is $9,992.42. Remember, though, that one day's worth of your session fee acts as your holding fee and is therefore credited toward your residuals. Holding fees can be applied to any media type, but only once per cycle. To account for this, we'll subtract $783.10 out of that total above, leaving you with $9,209.32. Add your full session fee to that number, and this job is worth $10,775.52. Not bad for a couple days' work!

Remember that this is for a 13-week cycle, so if they want to keep the spot running beyond that, they'll have to start the process over for the next cycle, which could be another 13 weeks, or it could be 4 weeks or 1 year. If they don't air the spot but still want the option to do so, they'll owe you a holding fee (equal to a scale session fee) every 13 weeks until they air it again, they release the spot (retire it forever), or until the MPU expires.

This example is useful to see how the higher end of the union commercial spectrum works, but there are a lot of ads that won't get that kind of airplay. Spots running locally and regionally don't generate that kind of money. I've made plenty of commercials that paid a session and a few hundred dollars' worth of use. If you booked one job that made $25,000 in a year, I would consider that a jackpot.

Remember that doing a union commercial means you'll be under a product conflict, meaning you won't be able to appear in commercials for competing products while the commercial is airing or you're receiving holding fees.

Nonunion Commercials

Typical nonunion commercials pay between $300 and $600 per spot for the session. Agents try to get buyout fees in place of residuals, but they're not always successful. If they are, your buyout could double or triple what you made for the session. In exchange for the buyout, they can air the spot everywhere as often as they want without making any additional talent payments. So if your session was $500 and your buyout was $1,500, your total earnings for that spot would be $2,000. Again, not bad for a day's worth of work in front of a camera.

Time limits are sometimes negotiated on usage, but often the advertiser wants to use the spot in perpetuity, otherwise known as forever. Some spots air for a while, go away, then come back years later. When this happens, agents will likely get in touch with the client to ask for more money, but the client is under no obligation to pay if it wasn't negotiated up front. There are no holding fees in the nonunion world.

There's a fast food chain in the Midwest that produced a commercial in the 1990s featuring a nonunion actor. At the time, no one knew him. He did the commercial, they paid him for his time, and both parties went their separate ways. Fast forward thirty years, and that unknown actor is now a big star. What does the company do? They take a still image from that old commercial and put it on their food trucks. Can they do that? It seems that they can since the commercial wasn't covered under a union contract. Maybe they paid him to use his likeness all these years later, maybe not. It's up to his representatives to contact the company for payment for this new use.

Free bargaining rules the nonunion roost. That means you and your agent can negotiate for as much as you can get for session fees, buyouts, lifts, and other kinds of uses. Usually advertisers who hire nonunion talent do so because it's a cost savings, not to mention that it doesn't come with the task of tracking where and how often a spot runs. Instead of adding a bunch of small fees together, they'll usually offer talent one flat fee for everything, leaving the actor to decide whether it's something they'd be willing to take.

This doesn't mean that nonunion actors get ripped off. Agents do their best to get rates comparable with union rates. Not every advertiser can pay those, though, and there are plenty of actors who are happy to accept lower compensation. Again, as you work, you'll start to decide which path is best for your career.

In some cases, the nonunion agent isn't the entity negotiating the actor's pay. Rates are sometimes agreed upon between clients and casting directors. So if you book a nonunion spot by auditioning at a casting director's office, it doesn't matter which agent you're with, you'll get the same deal as everyone else in town.

Industrials

If commercials are the gifts that keep on giving, industrials are the practical, useful gifts from your aunt Eleanor. They're not sexy, but you're glad to get them.

Because they're not broadcast, industrials don't trigger holding fees or other residuals. You only get your session fee, but the good news is that there are more opportunities to work in industrials than spots.

Industrials are usually much cheaper than commercials to produce, so more companies can afford to make them. Also, producers tend to be incredibly picky when it comes to casting their spots. They want just the right actor for every role. In contrast, there's less emphasis placed on the talent in industrials, and more placed on the message. Even if you're not perfect for the job, you're still in the running if you give a strong audition. Finally, hundreds of actors can be auditioned for a commercial. Industrials sometimes only audition four or five actors per role. All this means you've got a greater chance of being hired for an industrial than a commercial.

The union's industrial contract spells out different rates for different situations. There are two categories that all industrials fall into: Categories I and II. The distinction lies with the intended audience. Videos that are for the company's internal use only fall under Category I. These are usually training videos, or other productions that are not used to sell products, but to inform or otherwise advise the company's workforce about a certain product, policy, or issue. Anything that's produced with the intention of showing it to clients, potential customers, or anyone who does not work for the company falls into Category II. Those rates are a little higher than Category I because the actor's work could be exposed to more viewers.

Some smaller markets have waivers to these rules. The Chicago market, for example, has an exception that limits the use of Category II to the city and its collar counties. Industrials produced outside this area can only be paid at Category I rates. Remember that everything is negotiable, though.

The union's contract also considers what type of role an actor is playing. There are background actors, day players, and narrators. If you're a background player, you're an extra and don't have lines. You'll earn $161 for an eight-hour day whether the shoot falls into Category I or II. If you're a day player, you've been hired to play a role while not addressing the camera. For example, if you're hired to play a mechanic and your scene consists of a discussion between you and another actor playing the customer, you're both considered day players. The Category I day player rate is $617, and Category II is $768. A narrator's job is to look directly into the camera while delivering the script. The narrator scale is $1,122 and $1,331 per day for Categories I and II, respectively.

Recently, agents have been negotiating an additional fee if the video is intended to be publicly available online. These fees could increase your paycheck as much as 50 percent. If there's some additional aspect to the project, like a print shoot for online ads, there will be an extra fee for that use.

Last, most often the producer will ask actors to bring some wardrobe to industrial shoots. They'll want a selection of looks, so plan on bringing at least a few of whatever you're asked to bring. For your trouble you'll be paid $21 for each look that winds up on camera, which is intended to help offset the cost of dry cleaning.

You might think that industrials can be used forever, but you'd be wrong. They have a maximum period of use just like commercials. Category II projects can be used for three years, beginning ninety days after the last day of the project's production. After that, they must be renewed by negotiation. Category I projects can be used in perpetuity.

Nonunion industrial pay rates are a little lower, but not much. Years ago, my first multi-day industrial paid $250 per day. I was hired to play a college kid who needed training on how to use his library's new electronic card catalog (remember, this was before the internet was a thing). All my scenes were with another actor, who played the role of the nice librarian who had all the answers. We were both day players. If I were to get that same job today, it would probably pay around $400 per day. On-camera narrators get somewhere around $750 per day for their work, maybe more if they're very experienced, maybe less if the client's budget is tight.

These rates can fluctuate depending on the market the actor is in, and how well the nation's economy is doing. Smaller markets are more likely to offer actors less, and if there's any recession buzz or if unemployment is high, producers will try to get talent for as little as possible. That's part of their job. Our job is to try to get as much as we can.

Under certain circumstances, you are entitled to extra money in addition to your daily rate. If the industrial requires you to work longer than eight hours, you'll go into overtime, which means your rate increases. If you're required to travel to the location, all your expenses will be covered or reimbursed. If you're union, you'll even be given a per diem to cover the cost of eating while you're traveling.

Sometimes, however, nonunion producers don't have the budget to pay overtime or travel costs. In these situations, you should be notified beforehand so you can decide whether the job is worth doing. I've heard of nonunion jobs paying a flat rate no matter how long it takes to get the job done.

Voice Over

We can be hired to do a number of different kinds of VO work. Each area of voice over has its own goals, audiences, and talent buyers, and thus requires a specific skill set, not to mention home recording equipment.

TV and radio spots and longer narration work are very common jobs for actors, but that's not all we do. There are opportunities in audiobooks, video games, interactive displays, promos, radio station IDs, phone systems, animated programs and features, looping and dubbing, storecasting (those announcements at grocery stores touting the sale of the week), websites, toys and gadgets that use human voices. You're far less likely to come by these obscure kinds of jobs, and the rates for many of them are negotiated between agents and producers. For that reason, it would be impossible to discuss what you can earn doing them, so I'll stick to the mainstream work. For a more complete explanation of all VO genres, see *The Voice Over Startup Guide*.

TV spots can be a great source of income for voice talent. Union scale for a TV voice over session is $588.90 per spot. You'll notice that this is less than the scale session fee for on-camera work because you're less likely to be associated with a product (and thus less likely to become overexposed) just by the sound of your voice.

The union rates for voice over work follow the same system as on-camera work, but they're about 25 percent less. Using our previous example, if you voiced a spot at scale for a national retailer, you'd get $588.90 for the session. If they aired it thirteen times under the Class A network rates, you'd get $1,734.94 for the thirteen-run guarantee. If we did the math of everything else in our example and put it all together, we'd earn a little over $7,000 in residuals.

Crediting one holding fee per cycle also applies in VO. Also, if the spot isn't airing, they would owe holding fees every thirteen weeks until it started airing again. If you did two spots, your earnings would double. Obviously, the fees can add up to quite a nice chunk of change. Check out the current rates on SAG-AFTRA's website.

Radio spots pay a lot less than TV, but that doesn't mean you can't make good money in that medium. They're recorded under a different contract, one for audio commercials. Anything that's recorded for playback through an audio-only source falls under this contract and is commonly just called a radio spot, even if it's for something like Pandora or Spotify. Union scale for a radio session is $347.60 per spot. The spot can be run regionally for $1,138.24, and if it runs online for a year, the fee is $1,390.40. There are no holding fees (and no conflicts) in radio, but if your spot is renewed after its initial run of six months, you'll be paid another session plus usage.

When we talk about longer-form narration, we're usually referring to the industrial kind. Companies are always producing videos that need some kind of voice over narration, which is usually paid by the hour instead of by the job. Scale for this kind of session is $505 for the first hour and $148 for each additional half hour. That's for Category I, which we know is a project only to be viewed by the company's employees. Category II scale is $565 for the first hour and $148 for each additional half hour.

Like their on-camera counterparts, there are no residuals on industrial narration jobs, but sometimes agents can negotiate additional fees if the video will be made public online.

Nonunion agents try to negotiate a buyout for TV spots but aren't always successful. Expect to earn around $300 to $500 per spot, and possibly double that for a buyout that may last a year or more.

Nonunion radio payments are super straightforward. You get your session and that's it. Expect that payment to be $200 to $400 per spot. Buyouts are sometimes offered, but less often than with TV. There are no cycles to worry about in the nonunion world, so your session payment will be the last check you get for that spot.

Narration jobs are one area where nonunion talent can earn as much, or sometimes more than their union counterparts. Again, agents try to negotiate a session fee and a buyout for a set amount of time, especially if the project is going online. If they're successful, you can earn anywhere from $200 to $500 for the session, and maybe double that for the buyout.

Commercial Print

Most print jobs are paid by the hour, and many pay well, but not as well as on-camera or VO jobs. Where you might be able to earn about $300 for an hour of work doing a radio spot, that same hour spent working a print shoot for a catalog might pay $200.

Some print jobs pay a lot more than just an hourly rate. If the photos are going to be used for multiple media like online, in brochures, and on point-of-purchase displays, you may get usage fees in addition to your hourly rate. This is sort of like the union's residual system except it usually all comes at once instead of spread out over time.

I once did a job with five other actors for a company that makes backyard grills. I was booked for an afternoon, about four hours, and the shots were to be used for various marketing materials. The usage didn't include billboards or magazine ads, but they used them in pretty much every other media outlet for a term of two years. For that I got a flat rate of $1,100.

I've known actors who have earned a lot more from print jobs. I once had a meeting with an agent who was considering working with me for industrials. When I showed up to meet her, she welcomed me into the office and showed me to her desk, which was right next to another agent's desk. Turns out he ran the agency's print department. During my visit with the industrial agent, the print agent was visited by an actress who wanted to thank him for getting her a job. She was thrilled to have it, but she didn't know exactly how much she was going to make for it. The agent did some math and gave her the good news: she cleared $7,000 for the job! I thought, "Wow! What would I do with that kind of money?!"

She must have read my mind because the first thing she said was, "Great! Now I can pay my taxes." That sort of put the brakes on the celebration, but I was still amazed that you could earn that much just from getting your picture taken.

Trade Shows/Live Events

Expect a host to earn between $150 and $300 per day. Crowd gatherers will earn somewhere in the same range. Product specialists earn around $500 per day because they have more training and knowledge. Presenters are paid even more because it's harder to find people who have the unique mix of skills required for the job. Today's day rates for presenters are between $750 and $1,500. As my dad always said, that's better than a sharp stick in the eye.

There are other kinds of live corporate events in need of actors. These aren't trade shows, but more like special events that companies do either for their employees or the public. I once worked an investor meeting for a Fortune 500 company. Basically my job was to present information to hedge fund managers at certain times of the day. I had a script and instructions for what to say when I didn't know the answer to a question. Rates for these kinds of events vary widely and can be as little as $200 to over $1,000 per day.

There's no union that covers trade shows or other live events, so it's up to your agent to negotiate these rates. Occasionally clients will want to tape your performance for some reason, and you may get additional payment for the video. These videos count as industrials. If you're union, the contract will set the rates, and if you're nonunion, your agent will negotiate any additional money.

TV/Film

Student films, no-budget projects, and films on SAG waivers (agreements that adjust requirements for actor pay) won't pay much more than $100 per day, if they pay anything. Most of these auditions won't come through your agent since there's no chance they'll make a commission on them.

However, your agent will be the only way to get big-budget TV and film work. It will all be done under a SAG-AFTRA contract. The union has contracts for both TV and film, and as you can imagine, they have complicated payment structures. So complicated, in fact, that for me to give you hard numbers beyond simple day rates would be impossible. More on that in a minute.

If you're booked as a principal actor on a TV or film project, you'll be paid for the shoot day (the session), and you'll also get residuals for as long as the project is being reused. Book the right project, and most of your earnings will come from residuals.

Great jobs result in a nice stream of money for years. For work on a film, producers pay residuals if the movie is released in other places besides its original method of release. Think DVD, basic cable, online, or on free or subscriber-based television. For work on a television show, you'll be paid when the show starts reruns on its original broadcast network or is released to other media like streaming services. A popular movie or top-tier TV show can bring in quite a bit of money as it's reused by the producer or distributor. Principal performers will earn these residuals. Background players are paid only for their time on set.

Unfortunately, the complexity of the residual system in place for TV and film will make it impossible to get specific with numbers, so I'll do my best to explain how it works. I'm going to keep things as simple as I can. For that reason, you might find yourself wanting more information, which you can find on the SAG-AFTRA website.

There are actually two different formulas for calculating residuals for actors appearing in TV shows and movies. They're both based on your initial compensation for the project. In other words, the more you're paid at the time of the job, the higher your residuals will be.

Your compensation has a lot to do with the size of your role. In television, costars are the lowest on the pay scale. This is because these roles are usually functionary. They help move the story along, but it does not revolve around them like it might a guest star, which is the next level up. Guest stars are more central to the plot of the episode and might even play out a story that lasts over several episodes. At the top of the pay scale are the series performers, who appear in every episode of a show. Film roles are a little less clearly defined and are generally just broken down into leads and supporting players.

TV Formulas

Residuals can either be calculated using a fixed formula or one based on gross receipts of the project, meaning the amount the producers receive for the sale of that project. Most network TV shows follow the fixed residual formula, which simply means that every time your episode airs, you'll get a check for that airing.

Let's say you book a costar role that appears in one episode. The breakdown that comes with the audition will tell you what kind of role you're auditioning for, but there are some things that can clue you into the fact that it's a costar. If the role only has a few lines, shows up only in one scene, and doesn't have a character name in the script (it's just listed as "Bartender"), it's a costar.

Costars are usually hired by the day because often their scene can be shot and wrapped in less than eight hours. For that reason, they're sometimes called "day players." They get a minimum of $1,158 for one day of work in an hour-long show if they've never been hired in TV before. Once you have a job or two under your belt, your agent can sometimes negotiate a higher rate, also known as your quote. Your agent will try to get this for you, but they won't always be successful.

Whether you're booked at scale or at your quote, your session payment includes the episode's first run. Residual payments are triggered when the episode runs after that. The first time a broadcast episode reruns in its regular time slot (the second actual airing), you'll get a payment equal to half of a session fee. Beyond that, calculating residuals starts to get tricky. They're based on formulas that consider such variables as the contract in place at the time of the shoot, the production length and type, and the market where the show appears.

Let's assume your show has been sold into syndication, which means it's been bought by other broadcast networks to be aired in non-prime-time slots. The formula used to figure the residual payment for the episode takes into account the number of times you've already been paid. You'll earn 40 percent of the scale day rate for the first rerun, 30 percent for the second, 25 percent for the third, and on and on until the twelfth rerun. At that point, you'll earn a payment of 5 percent of scale every time the show airs thereafter.

There are also foreign residual fees, which means the show has been sold to a free TV network based outside of the US and Canada, and these payments are about 35 percent of a scale session fee. Also, remember that the value of residuals is tied to your initial compensation. If you booked a guest-starring role, the rates are higher, and thus the residuals would be higher as well.

These residuals are generally paid quarterly, though in my experience there can be variations in the length of time between payments. Some shows are right on time, every time, and others don't always meet deadlines. Eventually it all works out and you do get your money, and the union even operates a fund for residual payments that somehow get lost in the system.

Another TV Example

Network TV shows are great, but these days the majority of programs are made for streaming networks. They follow a different residual formula, one that pays less than the legacy networks. The same session fees are in place, but most high-budget shows on streaming platforms will calculate residual payments using something called the "distributor's gross receipts," which is the amount producers make by selling the show to a streaming service. This number varies from show to show, but the episode's cast will share about 3.6 percent of this amount. The variation means these residuals are harder to calculate and ultimately predict.

Let's assume you book a costar on an episode of a thirty-minute show that runs on a streaming video on demand, or SVOD, platform. According to the contract that governs cast payments for these platforms, figuring your residuals starts with determining your total actual compensation for the job.

If you were hired at scale for one day, you may have actually earned more than just your scale session fee. Your agent probably negotiated their commission into your deal, which adds 10 percent to your check. And if you're lucky enough to get your quote, maybe you worked for a few hundred dollars over scale. Your total session fee includes that additional money, and that number is used as the basis for your residual calculation.

In addition to paying you for the time on set, the session fee includes the first ninety days of the episode's exhibition. After that, a clock of sorts starts ticking. The show has to pay residuals as long as it is available for audiences to view. Here's where it gets tricky.

Every streaming platform requires subscribers to operate. They report how many they have to the union annually. That number is then used to calculate what's called the "subscriber factor," which is expressed as a percentage. The more domestic subscribers a platform has, the higher the factor. There are different percentage tiers, up to a 150 percent tier. This accounts for the fact that not all platforms have the same number of eyeballs potentially watching a show. Let's assume your steaming service's subscriber factor is 150 percent. You'd take your overall initial compensation and multiply it by 150 percent, and then take that number and multiply it again by something called your "year percentage."

The year percentage refers to how long it's been since the episode was first made available on the platform. The percentages decrease by about 5 percent every year, so the longer the show airs, the less you'll earn each year. Let's assume it's been one year since you shot the show. Your first year percentage is 45 percent. This amount will eventually get down to 1.5 percent in year thirteen, after which it stays there forever.

Scale for working one day on an episode of a show is currently $1,158. Scale plus a 10 percent agent fee comes to $1,273.80. Let's assume your booking was straightforward, and no additional fees were triggered (like overtime, meal penalties, or anything else). You were paid scale plus 10 percent, so that's your starting point for your residual calculation. The math looks like this:

Overall Initial Compensation x Subscriber Factor =

$1,273.80 x 150%= $3184.50

$3,184.50 x Year Percentage = Your Residual Payment for the Year

$3184.50 x 45%= $1433.03

Large platforms also offer foreign residuals, which are calculated in a similar way as domestic residuals. They are paid annually, which means you can expect to get one check that covers a year's worth of use.

AVOD Programming

AVOD stands for "Ad-supported Video On Demand." These plat-forms offer content that's free to viewers because it's paid for by commercials instead of subscriptions. Amazon's FreeVee is current-ly following this model, and it's likely we'll see more of this in the future.

Your initial compensation will cover 26 weeks of use on the platform, after which you'll start earning residuals, and they'll follow the TV formulas. If the show is moved to a platform with paid subscrip-tions, principal performers will share 3.6% of the distributor's gross receipts, and if it's moved to traditional media like network TV, residual formulas for that medium will apply.

Additional Residuals

There's another source of residuals related to shows that are made for streaming services, and that's the "success metric". Programs qualify for this bonus when they're viewed by 20% of a platform's subscriber base within the first 90 days they're available to on the platform.

This additional residual, which is over and above those already dis-cussed, doesn't go directly to the cast of these programs. The money is first deposited into a fund administered by SAG-AFTRA. 75% of it is to be split among the principal performers who appear in the shows that meet this bonus threshold. The rest of the money is to be distributed by the union in other ways.

This fund was just created in December of 2023 and is so new that the details are still being worked out. It remains to be seen how many projects will qualify for the bonus and how much additional money will be distributed to their casts. When more information becomes available, we'll post an explainer on ActingCareerMentor.com.

Film Formulas

Just like in TV shows and commercials, actors get session and residual fees when they appear in studio movies. Current scale for one day of work is $1,158 and $4,019 for a week.

Residual payments for film follow the revenue sharing method, where the entire cast splits some of the gross receipts when it gets distribution to various media outlets, but that's only when there's enough money to share with the cast. Some films don't make enough to trigger a revenue split.

When the residual kicks in, the calculations are even more complicated than they are for TV because they give weight to actors who were paid more at the time of production. Because of this, I won't be able to give you hard numbers, so I'll just give you the formula.

Film residuals are usually figured using the production's gross revenues after certain deductions are taken. That number is called the "adjusted gross." When there's enough revenue left over to share with the cast, the union uses a "time and salary" system, which is expressed in units, to figure out how to divide a portion of those revenues between cast members. The more time you spent on set and the more you earned for that time, the greater your share of the revenue split. A big cast means more actors to share the revenue, lowering each actor's individual take.

Currently, principal actors share 3.6 percent of the adjusted gross when the film airs on television or is moved over to a streaming platform after initial release. If the movie is released on Blu-Ray or DVD, the residual is 4.5 percent of the first million dollars of gross sales and 5.4 percent on the rest. Remember, principal actors share this number, not background players.

But not all films are shot under this particular agreement. The union has contracts for producers of independent films with much lower rates than the basic agreement. Depending on the budget, an actor could get as little as $100 per day under the ultra-low budget agreement. This agreement allows for residual payments for things like internet use, but the payments are very low. You can check out the details of this and other low-budget contracts at sagindie.org.

Action Items

Things you can do right now:

- Visit the SAG-AFTRA website and read up on requirements and costs to join.

- Also read about benefit programs, educational opportunities, and other benefits of membership.

- Download and explore the rate sheets for the different contracts.

- Subscribe to the SAG-AFTRA Foundation's YouTube Channel.

Chapter Seventeen

Additional Thoughts

E arlier I mentioned that lack of confidence can kill an actor's chances of developing a career. That's true, but it's not the only cracked rung on the ladder.

Actors are very good at getting in their own way. There are a host of mindset issues that can trip up progress, like comparing oneself to others, impostor syndrome, entitlement issues, and general self-sabotage.

There's one particularly nasty habit many actors develop, and that's being focused on results. Here's what it sounds like:

"I should be a series regular by now."

"I've booked fewer jobs this year than last."

"I've been acting for (insert number of years here) and I can't go full time yet."

"I've auditioned for the same casting office ten times and they've never booked me."

Depending on who's saying them, these things might be factually true. But they all reveal the actor's mindset, which is that there's something's wrong with their career trajectory. It's easy to see why actors think this way. We all want results and it can be frustrating when we don't see them. Problem is, when it comes to an actor's progress through the industry, there are no standards for fast or slow, right or wrong, normal or not.

Consider that progress can be measured in ways besides money and status. Instead, we can choose to look inward. There's always something new to learn. Once we've learned it, we can always improve. Are we doing what we can to absorb as much as possible and refine our mastery of our newfound skills? If we can honestly say that we are, then it doesn't matter where we are relative to the random person we met in our acting class. We're making solid progress.

One final pro tip: the easiest way to make sure you're continually learning is to surround yourself with people who are further along in their journey. Once you have a good base of training, join a class that's a level or two above where you are. Feeling like I have to play catch-up makes me work harder, and this is doubly true when others are watching. Aligning ourselves with stronger actors helps move us forward quicker than we could on our own. Remember, no one does anything in this business without some help from other people.

Progress can only be made if we stay in the game. Do you know how many people want to be actors? Tons. Just ask any agent. They'll tell you about the emails they get, the ones from the wives who want to get their husbands agents for their birthday, or from kids who aren't old enough to get themselves to auditions. The inboxes of talent agencies are overflowing with people wanting to follow a dream.

My first voice over teacher mentioned something that I still remember to this day. He said that the longer I stayed in the business, the more of a veteran of it I would become, even if I never worked a single job! He was adamant that a large part of this business is just showing up. It was his way of telling me that persistence would be the key to getting a career off the ground. Nothing is handed to us. The business makes us earn everything.

Sometimes it comes down to how much we want it. Do you want to be an actor? Then do it! There's a way forward, and you can find it. It doesn't have to be my way, or the one someone else shows you. In fact, the best way is probably the one you build yourself.

However you get it done, I hope I played a small role. Tradition says I'm supposed to wish you broken limbs, but I always thought that was a little silly. So I'll just sign off with a big ol' GOOD LUCK! May you always get what you deserve from this business.

Acknowledgements

I've been lucky enough to work with an amazing community of people. Many thanks to the hundreds of actors, teachers, agents, clients, casting professionals, and students who have played various roles in my acting journey. Without them, I'd be doing something else for a living and I'd probably be super unhappy doing it. I'm extremely appreciative to my editor, Elizabeth Oliver. Patricia, my wife, continually shines her light on our family, and I can't thank her enough.

Lastly, I want to thank people like YOU. The curious, the dreamers, the practical, the right-brained, the left-brained, the folks who don't believe they can do it, the ones who know they're destined for greatness, and those who just want the chance to get there. Your questions were the driving force behind this and all the other books I've written. I'm so grateful that you have trusted me to guide you through this industry.

Excerpt from The Voice Over Startup Guide

Y ou might think your voice is the thing you'll use most as a voice over talent, but you'd be wrong. It's your ear.

If you've ever seen footage from a rock concert, you may have noticed band members wearing in-ear monitors on stage. They look like hearing aids. They serve two functions: to protect musicians' hearing and to allow them to hear themselves relative to the rest of the band. Without that feedback, the noise of the concert would make it impossible to hear their own performance, leaving them with no hypothetical target to aim at. They'd have no idea if they were in time, in tune, or not.

Your ear is the key to how you sound because it allows you to monitor yourself and those around you. As a voice actor, you need to be good at listening. Humans primarily rely on their sight to get them through the day, but our hearing is a close second. We just need to refine that sense as it applies to voice over.

There are three points in time when this will be especially important: when you're learning to identify different styles of reading out loud (known as reads), when you're doing your own reads, and when you're being asked to adjust your reads to give your client something they need. If you can't monitor feedback and adjust accordingly at any of those points, this career is going to be a struggle.

Identifying Read Styles

Let's start with commercials. That's my specialty and a subject I like to make videos about, but it's also a basic skill. Every voice talent should be able to analyze ad copy (scripts written by commercial copywriters) and come up with a good commercial read.

Maybe you've never really listened to commercials before. You've heard them, but listening is different. Hearing is like glancing at a painting and noticing it's a landscape. Listening is noticing that it brings you somewhere. Maybe it reminds you of your childhood or a favorite vacation destination. Taking the analogy further, listening critically means leaning in close enough to see the brushstrokes so you understand how the artist created the image and why it made you feel what you felt.

We want to listen for that level of detail in commercials. We're going to look for the brushstrokes in the voice over.

There's a great site called iSpot.tv that archives thousands of commercials, and I like to use it as a research tool. Take thirty minutes, go there, and browse ads. I'll wait.

Close your eyes while you play some commercials (called spots in the ad world) and just listen. After a while you'll notice they don't just sound different; they have moods. Like paintings, they conjure different emotions. Some make you smile; others intrigue you. The combination of what's being said and how the voice actor is saying it adds up to something you can describe. As you listen, try to pick out attitudes the talent adopts as they're reading.

Friendly. Aspirational. Confident. Secretive. Tempting. Knowledgeable. Excited.

Need a few examples? Sure thing. Below is a collection of commercial copy with a description of the read style that made it to air. All of them are rewritten versions of actual commercials. As much as I would like to use the original scripts and audio from those spots, copyrights and trademarks prevent me from doing so. Instead, I've modified the copy and replaced every brand name with a generic one: "Harry's." You'll see that Harry's sells everything from skin care to SUVs.

If you haven't already, now's the time to visit Complete-Voiceover .com to get the free audio files associated with all the examples in this book. You'll be able to listen to a performance of each script. Combining reading with listening will be the best and fastest way to learn.

Here's a friendly read.

Example 1a

Here's to making your mornings just a little better.

199

```
The sweet, savory, egg and cheese croissant sand-
wich.

Breakfast. At Harry's.
```

This guy is friendly and knowledgeable.

Example 1b

```
Jason knows how to keep his wheels spinning.

That's why he starts his day with those famous
scoops.

And delicious, heart healthy oatmeal.

By taking steps to lead a healthy lifestyle, Jason
knows he'll be ready for life's curveballs.

Harry's oatmeal. And try oatmeal crunch with nutty
oat clusters.
```

Take a listen to someone who is folksy and trustworthy.

Example 1c

```
We know the value of trust.

We built our business on it.
```

Back when the country went west for gold, we were the ones who carried it back east.

Over the years, we built on that trust.

We always made that effort.

Today we still operate the same way.

Trust. In your hands.

Here's a guy who's compassionate.

Example 1d

Mike woke up with a sore knee. But he's got work to do.

He can't afford to miss today's deadlines.

He relies on Harry's to get past the pain, and get him through the day.

If he'd taken anything else, he be taking more pills right now.

Only Harry's has the strength to stop tough pain all day long.

No other pain reliever can do that.

Harry's. Relief, all day long.

And here's a read with quiet confidence.

Example 1e

```
At Harry's, we turn emotions into jewelry.

Jewelry that tells her you never want to let her
go.

In a way that's so much more than words.

It could be a piece our designers created for our
exclusive collections.

Or it could be something made just for her.

The one gift that tells her exactly how you feel
about her.

That's Harry's.
```

This talent is simply wowed by everything she's saying.

Example 1f

```
Do you dread shopping for jeans?

Are you fed up with jeans that just don't fit?

Introducing Harry's Jeans.
```

The super cute, one size fits always denim.

It's a customized, perfect fit for every woman, every shape, every time.

No matter the size, Harry's Jeans will always fit you perfectly!

Finally, this read has a little wink of shared knowledge to it.

Example 1g

Blind dates can feel uncomfortable enough.

Your clothes shouldn't add to the problem.

Harry's. The most comfortable.

By now you realize there are a million ways to interpret ad copy, but they're all useless if you can't tell the difference between them. If you're asked to sound like you're sharing a secret with a friend but you instead do a straight announce read, you will not get that job. When you train your brain to listen critically, you'll be able to describe reads in terms of how they make you feel, identify the attitude the talent was trying to convey when they spoke, and apply that to your own reads.

Once you're really paying attention, you'll recognize shifts within reads. Sometimes attitudes change from one moment to the next. Let me show you what I mean. Wells Fargo Bank recently aired a commercial that got a lot of attention. The entire spot is driven by the VO, and it's amazingly well done. It's so good that I made a video about it on my YouTube channel, where I break down the read line by line.

The copy begins by describing the company's history. There's a quiet pride in the talent's voice as he moves through the years. Then, twenty-two seconds into the spot, he sounds ever so mildly taken by surprise when he says the company lost their way. And as he continues to tell the story, he is ever more hopeful, quietly excited to share all the changes the company is committed to making. The read crescendos, like a concerto, until he's halfway begging us to believe him when he says, "Because earning back your trust is our greatest priority." Then he backs off, and lands the spot barely impressed with the notion of rebirth. He just tells it like it is: "Established 1852. Re-established 2018." The subtext? You trusted us back then, and you can still trust us today.

He never gets much above a whisper. He doesn't need to add volume; he makes his point through pacing, inflections, pauses, and rhythm. He doesn't over enunciate or change his personality. He is the same guy through it all and makes microadjustments to push all those emotional buttons. Bravo to all involved.

Does it surprise you there's this amount of detail in commercial reads? It shouldn't. Hundreds of thousands of dollars are spent on commercials. Advertisers and their ad agencies want a return on their investment. Their message has to be 100 percent clear, no matter if the client spent ten thousand or ten million dollars, and the talent's read can be a huge part of the success or failure of that message.

Because a lot is riding on the success of any voice over job, decision makers put a lot of trust in their voice talent. It's a big responsibility, so I can't overstate the importance of knowing how to build reads that make sense for the job on which you've been hired.

Your Reads

I chose commercials as a starting point because it's so easy to find examples of good work, but there are a couple exercises that'll help you develop a feel for reading in any category: promos, audiobook narration, e-learning, etc.

Because voice over is mostly a solitary business, voice actors self-direct. When you're new to the business, you can jump-start your training by finding inspiration in the reads that are already out there. So give this a try: choose a script from the previous pages, and read it with several different attitudes or intentions. Start with friendly and knowledgeable, then move on to happy and excited, then be absolutely wowed by what you're saying, then read it with the voice of authority. Always try to tell a story with the copy.

That idea, of being a storyteller first and foremost, will carry you far in this business and keep your career rolling.

***The Voice Over Startup Guide* is available on Amazon, Audible, and with local booksellers.**